LA   OD

YT

LANGUAGE LOGIC & GOD

FREDERICK FERRÉ

UNIVERSITY OF CHICAGO PRESS
Chicago and London

TO MY FATHER
from whom I heard my
first theological language

in love and respect

The University of Chicago Press, Chicago 60637
The University of Chicago Press, Ltd., London

© 1961 by Frederick Pond Ferré
All rights reserved. Published 1961
University of Chicago Press Edition 1981

Printed in the United States of America

85 84 83 82 81   1 2 3 4 5

Library of Congress Cataloging in Publication Data

Ferré, Frederick.
  Language, logic, and God.

  Originally published in 1961 by Harper, New York.
  Bibliography: p.
  Includes index.
  1. Logical positivism.   2. Languages—Philosophy.   3. Theology—
20th century.   I. Title.
  B824.6.F45   1981   200'.1'4   80-27305

  ISBN: 0-226-24456-3 (pbk.)

CONTENTS

PREFACE

THIS BOOK is an attempt to fill the present striking need for an introduction to contemporary linguistic philosophy as it bears on theological discourse. Wherever I have gone, recently, among educated Christians in Britain and America, I have encountered profound curiosity—and a good deal of anxiety—concerning modern methods in philosophy as they relate to the logical nature and validity of theological affirmations. Similarly I have found many of my students in contemporary philosophy and in the philosophy of religion becoming deeply absorbed in the issues raised by a critical examination of theological speech. From both groups, the intellectually alert Christians and the thoughtful graduate and undergraduate students of philosophy and religion, I have been heavily bombarded with appeals for direction to some book which would (1) set forth the central issues and arguments concerning theological discourse for readers who have familiarity with traditional philosophy but who are relatively untrained in contemporary philosophical practices and (2) place into perspective the present state of philosophical and theological discussion in this area of burgeoning interest. To my frustration, I have had to answer such requests with the admission that no such book exists and with the promise that I would try, some day, to provide that book myself. In preparing this volume, therefore, I have done my best to keep those promises in mind.

A word or two here concerning my use of the phrase "theological language" may prevent misunderstanding later. I do *not* employ this phrase in its narrow sense to refer merely to the discourse of academic theologians. I want it to be taken in its most inclusive sense, referring both to the language of theologians in their studies and to the speech of worshipers in pulpit or pew. Wherever we find words-about-God (theo-logy) we shall call it theological language. Some such general term is needed to span later distinctions which we may wish to make between the "language of living faith" ("religious language") and the "language of academic theology" ("systematic language").

I am heavily indebted to others for the help I have been given in writing this book and in doing the research which lies behind it. Most of my basic reading was done in Britain thanks to a Fulbright grant and an additional renewal grant administered by the unflaggingly helpful officials (now friends) at the United States Educational Commission in the United Kingdom. Additional financial assistance was provided by the National Council on Religion in Higher Education through the Kent Fellowship program. The University of St. Andrews, Scotland, was an ideal spot for my research, and my thanks are warmly extended to that institution for nurturing my studies under the kindly direction of Professor Edgar P. Dickie and for submitting my results to the critical scrutiny of Professors A. D. Woozley and J. O. Urmson.

Another whose wisdom has benefited my thoughts on the subject of this book is Professor John J. Compton, my former teacher, now colleague and treasured friend. He has given, in his characteristically unstinting way, vastly helpful criticism and encouragement. Since I have sometimes gone against his counsel, he cannot be blamed for the defects which remain in my finished work; but I should hate to imagine how much less satisfactory this book would have been without his help.

Thanks are also due Miss Maija Kibens and Miss Judith Anne Kolb for their stalwart help with proofs and index.

Finally I must somehow find words enough in our language to thank my wife for her part in this study. It will not be easy, for not only has she done supremely well all those wifely things which author-husbands seem to need but also she has typed draft after experimental draft of manuscript and cheerfully has hacked her way through the impenetrable jungle of my handwritten pages. Luckily, she knows how grateful I am; I needn't try to put it all down here.

F. F.

1

THE "FAMILY BACKGROUND" OF LINGUISTIC PHILOSOPHY

IN ORDER TO understand what linguistic philosophy has to say about theological discourse it is essential that the movement as a whole be brought into focus. The reader should be alerted to the fact, however, that some philosophers warn us away from the entire attempt. Antony Flew, for example, objects that it is "difficult" and "ultimately misleading" to try to isolate a linguistic philosophy;[1] and it is true that there is considerable diversity (as well as a deliberate attempt to avoid becoming merely another "school") among philosophers of language.

Despite these warnings, there are in fact enough areas of agreement among modern practitioners of linguistic analysis to justify viewing them as a loosely knit group rather than a sheer hodgepodge about whom nothing in general can meaningfully be asserted. Borrowing a concept used by Ludwig Wittgenstein in another context, we might say that the impression of unity given by linguistic philosophers is that of "family" resemblances, "for the various resemblances between members of a family: build, features, colour of eyes, gait, temperament, etc. etc. overlap and criss-cross in the same way. . . ."[2]

In large part the family background of contemporary philosophical thought reflects one of the most striking occurrences in modern intellectual history: the breakaway of the special sciences from the maternal leading strings of philosophy. "Mother" philosophy, when one by one her intellectual offspring established their separate households and began to thrive in their clearly defined independence, was left to ponder moodily her own future. Did any further function remain to her, or was her creativity now spent in nurturing the sciences into autonomy?

The nearly unanimous answer of modern philosophers to this crucial question is that philosophy's distinctive role has at last been revealed and clarified. As never before in history, and largely thanks to the departure of the sciences, philosophy has been freed to become what it always ought to have been and always has been when true to its own essential role.

I

It was quickly noticed that all the special sciences boasted a distinctive subject matter within relatively well-defined working limits. Could philosophy, too, find any special realm of empirical fact which it might claim as its province? If so, then its justification for existence would be established. But whichever way the philosopher turned in the empirical world, some special science was found already to be occupying the premises. Even the philosopher's apparent stronghold in "mental fact," on which philosophy had relied since Locke, was lost to the new science of psychology. "Psychology is no nearer related to philosophy, than is any other natural science."[3]

The shock of finding himself without any sphere of empirical subject matter to call his own left a deep mark on the philosopher of the early twentieth century; and contemporary philosophy of language owes a first principle of its thought to the slow and painful realization of earlier philosophers that, as Wittgenstein states it, "philosophy is not one of the natural sciences."[4]

The first principle so learned we may state as follows: *philosophy qua philosophy is empirically uninformative.*

Whatever philosophy's essential task might be (if it has one), it is not to compete with the trained and specialized scientists in their job of describing the structure and functioning of the world. Should a philosopher devote himself to empirical investigation, he would be acting no longer as a philosopher but (depending on the subject matter studied) as a botanist, astrophysicist, or psychologist.

If "philosophy was not a science alongside the natural sciences,"[5] then was it no longer a useful occupation of the modern age? What possible justification for its continued existence could be offered?

And if philosophy's study was not about the empirical world, what could it be about?

Kant's critique of reason was too well remembered to admit serious claims that philosophy's sphere of knowledge should be "transcendent" reality somehow "behind" the world of the sciences. The status of ethics, furthermore, and other "realms of value" was altogether too controversial—and suspiciously closely associated with psychology—to appear promising as a secure foundation for philosophical endeavor. And to attempt to set up philosophy as co-ordinator of the sciences, "synthesizing" into one grand symphony of knowledge all the lesser themes of the special sciences, was tempting as an ideal; not only did it smack too much of Hegelian metaphysics, however, but also it looked like a hopeless task, demanding encyclopedic mental capacity far beyond the range of human powers even while offering no grain of hope that such a synthesis could be accomplished for the sometimes contradictory claims of the sciences in their present state of development.

With these alternatives ruled out, the opening of a "new" sphere came as a revelation to philosophers searching for the proper area of activity. This sphere was that of *meaning*. Philosophy would not have to do with meaning as the psychologist's "mental fact" (as in "I mean to swim the Channel") but with meaning in another sense, as logical *meaningfulness*. Such meaningfulness is that utilized somehow by language in its capacity to communicate; indeed, it is only in the realm of linguistic signification that this meaningfulness can be found and studied in its most highly developed form. Thus the factual statements of the empirical scientist are of interest to the philosopher, whose job it is to show in what way the language of the scientist communicates; but the goal of the philosopher's work is not to add one more item to the total of empirical knowledge. He is not concerned with the factual business of tracing the development of languages with the etymologist or of reporting linguistic usage with the lexicographer. His responsibility, instead, is the logical task of clarifying and illuminating the ends of language and the ways in which language is able to achieve these ends. The modern philosopher will scrutinize critically all statements—those made by mathematicians, theologians, philosophers, and others, past and present—bringing his new techniques to bear on them as well.

We may thus distinguish another basic principle of postwar linguistic philosophy. It is: *linguistic significance is the primary subject matter of philosophy*. This, like the principle asserting the empirical uninformativeness of philosophy, has become in practice so widely accepted that it is possible for Professor Gilbert Ryle to assert that "The story of twentieth-century philosophy is very largely the story of this notion of sense or meaning."[6]

Once stated, it soon became obvious to many philosophers that this understanding of the proper subject matter of philosophy was "new" in its self-conscious explicitness only. The history of philosophy since the time of Socrates, whose passionate interest was in the meaning of "justice," "knowledge," and "good," could be interpreted as a quest for meaning. Clearly the self-understanding of traditional philosophy was not entirely alien to the new formulation of philosophy's sphere of interest.

II

We shall have to postpone closer study of "meaning" as it is used here until later chapters, where differences within linguistic philosophy over the meaning of "meaning" will be encountered; but, despite important differences which will appear, today's linguistic philosophy has learned to find the *unit* of meaning not in the individual word so much as in the proposition or statement.

It was early evident that to abolish the psychological "idea" or "image" as an object of philosophical study was to go beyond the discrete word as the basic unit of meaning. Some words may evoke images and so have "psychological meaning," but the study of logical significance must go far beyond this consideration. The word alone remains incomplete—an abstraction—apart from the context of the proposition in which it plays a part. The older theory, accepting words as somehow "atoms of meaning" which are strung together to compose sentences, may at first sight seem adequate when examples are limited to concrete nouns and some verbs, but beyond this it runs into fatal difficulties. Confronted by abstract nouns, it must admit that their meaning is ultimately dependent on sentences defining them; even more strikingly such words as "if," "and," "or," and "not" are totally dependent for their significance on the functions they play in the wider context of the complete proposition. It would not normally be denied that words as such possess meaning of some kind (although J. L. Evans goes so far as to claim that "it is only in the context of a sentence that a word is meaningful,"[7] and Wittgenstein much earlier asserted, "Only the proposition has sense; only in the context of a proposition has a name meaning"[8]), but such meaning is of a fragmentary kind apart from its employment in the statement. The word serves as a sign, and most words are fully capable of signifying only in combination with other signs. Furthermore, the fact that the proposition is alone capable of truth or falsity (individual words cannot be true or false outside a propositional context) is another indication that the sort of meaningfulness vested in words is abstract and partial.

Sense and senselessness belong where truth and falsity belong, namely to complete sentences or statements. The meanings of subordinate parts of speech are abstracted features of what is or might be conveyed by full sentences, not pieces out of which the meanings of sentences are composed.[9]

Although occasional voices are raised in protest, contemporary linguistic philosophy accepts as fundamental the principle: *the proper locus of meaning is the proposition or statement.*

III

All the recognized sciences were not only explorers of a special subject matter but also possessors of a special method or methods developed to deal with their particular fields of study. A clearly defined methodology, indeed, seemed even more than a distinct subject matter to be the primary criterion of all the genuine intellectual disciplines.

Consequently the moment could not be long delayed when philosophers would challenge one another, and be challenged by their new academic colleagues, especially the natural scientists, to state unequivocally what sort of an enquiry philosophy was and what were the canons of its special methods, if it possessed any such methods.[10]

The reply was soon forthcoming: philosophy's method, appropriate to its own goals, must be *analysis*. Synthesis, or putting together, might have been a possible method for philosophers who imagined themselves to have some sort of self-subsistent, empirical subject matter, but the new understanding of the object of philo-

sophical concern eliminated that method. Meaningful statements
are (by definition) already unities. Only the method of picking
apart, or analysis, would be applicable to this subject matter. We
shall find various interpretations of the proper analytical procedure
when we distinguish differences within the larger "family" of linguistic philosophy; at the moment we are solely concerned with
their agreements. And here, without doubt, was a firm platform of
unanimity: *the function of philosophy is to engage in analysis of
the meaning of language.*

The early analyses of Russell, Moore, and others showed clearly
that great scope existed for philosophy under this new understanding of its function. Ordinary language is a subtle and sometimes
misleading instrument; meanings are elusive, often hidden or confused by the language which seems to express logically acceptable
propositions. Many systematically misleading expressions[11] haunt
the avenues of daily speech. Grammatically perfect sentences, as
we shall see, may conceal logical unmeaning. However much linguistic philosophers may otherwise disagree, they are one in the
conviction that there is likely to be something problem-causing
about unanalyzed language which proper analysis can remove.[12] In
the chapters to follow we shall be offered a number of examples of
this conviction.

Again let it be noticed that the conception of philosophy as
analysis may be presented, not with the motive of sweeping away
all that goes under the title of "the history of philosophy," but as
a clear formulation of what the greatest philosophers have, in fact,
been engaged in, though often with a dim awareness of the
real nature of their activities. As A. J. Ayer asserts, "I think it
can be shown that the majority of those who are commonly supposed to have been great philosophers were primarily not meta-
physicians but analysts."[13] Ayer then cites Locke, Berkeley, Hume,
Hobbes, Bentham, J. S. Mill, Plato, Aristotle, and Kant as examples
of misunderstood (at times self-misunderstanding) philosophical
analysts.

If analyzing philosophers should be challenged as to why they
consider such work to be worth while, some might reply that the
clarification of understanding needs no further justification, that
it shows itself intrinsically worthy. Others, pointing to the recent
history of physics, would appeal to the fact that clarification of

THE "FAMILY BACKGROUND" OF LINGUISTIC PHILOSOPHY   7

language must be of immense aid to the working scientist who is impatient of being imprisoned in avoidable linguistic pitfalls and is eager for help in distinguishing real problems, open to his empirical techniques, from empty linguistic confusions to which there can be no conclusive solution. Indeed, they may point out, scientists themselves (Einstein a leading example) have become increasingly aware of the importance of the meaning of their language. Still other philosophers might answer that their work at last was cleansing philosophical wheat from the chaff of ages and finally was establishing philosophy as an important branch of learning with a determinate job to do and a clear method of judging its success or failure.

2

THE LOGIC OF
VERIFICATIONAL ANALYSIS

VERIFICATIONAL ANALYSIS, as I should like to christen one of the two major movements which one may distinguish within the modern philosophical "family," takes distinctive positions on the nature and purpose of language, on the meaning of "meaning," and on the proper methods of philosophical analysis.* I shall state these positions, which are not my own, as sympathetically as possible before presenting, in the following chapter, an application of these views to theological discourse.

I

Language, verificational analysis insists, is essentially an instrument for the communication of fact or for the establishment of verbal conventions.

Shortly we shall examine what "communicating facts" involves, since this will be of importance for our understanding of "meaning" and "analysis," but first we are required to clarify the role of language in establishing verbal conventions. If language is to be useful in the former activity (however defined), its many terms or signs must bear some definite and dependable relationship to one another. If the elements of language were constantly shifting in their manner of working together, we should find ourselves in a strange Alice in Wonderland world where communication would

---

* It should be noted that all so-called "logical positivists" would, on my usage, be verificational analysts but that not all verificational analysts need be "logical positivists"—a genuine logical positivist being increasingly difficult to find today.

be impossible. (In the same way, if in a game all the rules were permitted to shift and vary, the point of the game—the playing of it—would be lost.) It is obvious, therefore, that language must be able to set rules for its employment; that is, a preliminary but vital function of language is to mark clearly the "ground rules" of the "game" by fixing the conventions which must hold if factual communication is to be possible.

Some of these conventions may take the form of setting up equivalences between signs; some may take the form of establishing the logical powers or functions of certain terms (like "if," "then," "and," "or," and "not"), thereby marking out the rules to be followed in logical inference. Some may show themselves quite obviously "conventional," as in the "explicit definitions"[1] of our dictionaries (especially where new technical terms are introduced), while others, perhaps the conclusions of complicated inferences, may surprise us and actually appear to us as discoveries. But we must not be misled by the *psychological* fact of our learning what we did not know before into the *logical* mistake of believing that we are discovering new fact; the appearance of factual discovery is illusory since whatever we "get out" of our rules for using language has been implicitly "put into" our rules when we initially "decided" to use them. When this is the case—when, that is, a proposition may be said to be true thanks solely to the meaning of the terms which constitute it—our proposition is said to be a "tautology" and language is used "analytically." The statement "My sister is a female sibling" is analytically true, for example, since simply to understand the meaning of the words which compose that sentence is to be aware of the truth of the statement expressed in a way quite different from the way we become aware of the truth or falsity of a non-analytic statement like "My sister is a blue-eyed blonde."

Not only may there be analytic statements which are thus "logically true," or tautologies, but conversely there are "logically false" combinations of signs, or contradictions (e.g., assertions about "four-sided triangles"), which can under no circumstance be true. Any meaningful proposition which is not a contradiction may be a "logical possibility," whether or not it is a *practical* possibility. It is a *logical* possibility, for example, to observe directly the surface of Venus (not now a practical possibility) or—to choose a different sort of logical possibility—to have sensations of an entirely (unimaginably) different kind from those made practical possibilities by the possession of human sense organs. That these logical possibilities are not practical possibilities is contingent, respectively, on technological and physiological *fact*. And upon the introduction of questions of fact, a wholly new set of critical procedures and criteria become relevant, toward which logical possibility and impossibility, tautology and contradiction are equally indifferent.

A crucial property of all language used analytically, then, is that no fact or experience whatever can have the slightest chance of upsetting our verdict of truth or falsity, because this verdict (by definition) depends on the proper use of language *and on nothing else*. To say this, however, is not to denigrate the importance of analytic statements; we are far from being fully aware of the consequences of our linguistic conventions and logical rules, and the whole responsibility of the study of logic is to bring interesting and useful information about such matters to our attention. Tautologies are compatible with any state of affairs and thereby empirically uninformative ("The propositions of logic therefore say nothing,"[2] says Wittgenstein provocatively), but this is not to say that all logical and mathematical studies of tautologies are unilluminating.

When we say that analytic propositions are devoid of factual content, and consequently that they say nothing, we are not suggesting that they are senseless. . . . For, although they give us no information about any empirical situation, they do enlighten us by illustrating the way in which we use certain symbols.[3]

Discoveries in the complexities of formal relationships provide the joints and muscles, furthermore, on which language may efficiently and confidently move. And in providing such joints and muscles there is real scope for creativity. "For a well-chosen definition will call our attention to analytic truths, which would otherwise have escaped us. And the framing of definitions which are useful and fruitful may well be regarded as a creative act."[4]

If analytic propositions supply a firm skeleton for language, propositions asserting some state of affairs clothe language with its flesh. This second activity of language, making use of "synthetic" propositions, is acknowledged by verificational analysis as its primary end, the end for which analytic statements serve as means.

"The essential business of language," declares Bertrand Russell, "is to assert or deny facts."[5]

The fact-asserting synthetic statement, in contrast to the analytic statement, does not depend for its truth or falsity on the meaning of its constituent symbols but rather on the extralinguistic data which it alleges to be the case. If I say, "Rain is a form of precipitation" (a statement which is analytically true), I am in no danger of being proved wrong by a look out of the window; you can prove me wrong only by finding that I am breaking the rules which govern the use of the terms involved. But if I say, "It is raining outside," it would be futile to try to discover whether or not I am making a true statement by looking into your dictionary! To check that statement you must look out of the window or go out and stand in the garden. More precisely, you must test its truth against some form of relevant *experience*. And in so far as it is only through our senses that we can gain information about reality outside our own minds, the truth test of our statement must be in terms of some actual or possible sense-experience.

Now we are in possession of a criterion whereby we may distinguish between analytic and synthetic statements: the truth or falsity of the former has no relevance to experience but is clearly determinable from examination of the terms involved in the statement; the latter may be shown true or false only by reference to some sense-experience which they promise to be obtainable. Since analytic statements can deal with the truths of logic or "relations of ideas" and synthetic statements are capable of asserting all possible "matters of fact" (to use Hume's classical distinction), verificational analysis concludes that within the synthetic-analytic dichotomy all logically important meaningfulness is included.

II

Turning to the theory of meaning, we must examine more carefully the logical structure of sentences used to express facts or establish verbal conventions—the two proper functions of language.

As to analytic meaning, little more need be said. Tautologies are meaningful in their uninformative way on the basis of the arbitrary or historically conventional decisions which they reflect. They are meaningful as notations of relationship between signs, however complex and interesting the form of these notations may become, not as "asserting or denying facts."

Our prime interest here, consequently, is in the meaning of statements other than tautologies. What is the essential meaning which synthetic propositions convey? One striking reply of verificational analysis is: *the meaning of a sentence is the method of its verification.*[6] Thus baldly stated, this explanation of the nature of factual meaning may seem startling and implausible, but let us examine it more closely.

In the first place we should note that any philosophical account of meaning is bound to seem odd to us so long as we are unwilling to involve ourselves in strictly philosophical categories of thought. Here "meaning" is understood as *logical equivalence,* a phrase which should become clear as we proceed. Despite the fact that philosophy has turned over to psychology the task of discovering and describing the "mental facts" associated with meaning, we still seem to crave from philosophy a theory of meaning which deals with "mental happenings" or "inward intent." Philosophy's job, however, is to philosophize, not to repeat the research of the psychologist; the philosophical theory of meaning will involve different considerations from either those of modern mental science or those of pre-analytical philosophy of former days. "Meaning" today, we should note, is, as A. J. Ayer points out, "a highly ambiguous symbol."[7]

This consideration at once helps us to look at the suggested theory of meaning with new appreciation. The philosopher is not trying to tell us that in making a statement we are "secretly" or "deep down" intending to refer to the methods of that statement's verification. On the contrary, it makes not a particle of difference whether we have any knowledge (subconscious or otherwise) of the manner of verifying that statement; its meaning in the philosophical sense is quite unaffected. We may not *know* the philosophically interesting meaning of our sentence otherwise, but perhaps it is the case that at times we are in fact largely ignorant of the meaning (that is, of the logical equivalents) of our utterances.

What, then, we may properly ask, is the philosopher trying to tell us when he makes the startling announcement that the meaning of non-analytic propositions is the methods of their verification? He is trying simply to say that his formula, the "verification principle" of meaning, shows us the way in which we should translate the sentence in question into other sentences referring directly to some logically possible experience. These derivative sentences about direct experiences (sometimes called "protocol-statements") need no further explanation or justification. When taken together with certain rules of inference they are equivalent "in use" to what was stated in symbolic shorthand by the original proposition.

The meaning of a sentence, for the philosopher, is therefore not to be equated with any mental facts about the speaker but is, rather, the *matter expressed by the sentence*, and ultimately is this content as it is translatable into logically connected statements referring directly to concrete experience obtainable through the senses.

Perhaps our earlier illustration of a synthetic sentence ("It is raining outside") could be used here to clarify this philosophical concept of meaning. If we were interested in this statement from the viewpoint of psychology we might probe "what I meant" by having said such a thing at the time I said it. For psychology it would be relevant to inquire whether or not I had learned the English language well enough to be aware of what I was saying (and how I had learned it), to inquire into my motives in uttering it (did I "mean" that our picnic would have to be canceled?) and into many other data concerning my mental condition. But the meaning of this sentence for the philosopher would be none of these bits of factual information; instead, his job would be to draw up a list of the empirical tests by which the content of my sentence could be translated into "protocol-statements" dealing with experience. We mentioned two of these possible "methods of verification" earlier: to look out of the window (possible approximation of a protocol-statement: "I see water falling there") or to stand in the garden (possible protocol-statement: "I feel wetness here"). Many more possible means of verification might be suggested, such as listening for the sound of raindrops on the roof, examining competent witnesses, and so on. Then when we ask the verificational analyst what "It is raining outside" *means,* he can supply the meaning of the statement by offering us these tests as procedures for seeing for ourselves in straightforward experiential terms what facts are being asserted or denied.

Such an example as the one here used offers both helpful and confusing features. It is helpful in that it is drawn from a scene where the methods of verification and rules of inference are familiar and employed by us all; but it may tend to be *too* easy and familiar a sentence, one whose methods of verification we have all utilized countless times and one which, therefore, it seems silly to labor over in this manner. The proposition here is so well known that it instantly suggests to us the possibilities for obtaining experience from it and the nature of the experiences to be expected. This need not always be the case, however; turning to the more abstruse reaches of any science the layman will find statements whose meaning is far from self-evident. What does a physicist mean when he says that the notion of absolute simultaneity is no longer tenable? We are directed by verificational analysis to the methods which he uses to show that time is relative to systems of motion and thus directed ultimately to particular statements reporting sense experiences derived (or derivable) from experiments with "atomic clocks," rapidly moving earth satellites, and so on. Here the verificational analyst's help may be seen in its full usefulness; he offers us a program for dispelling our confusion or ignorance of meaning by asking for translations, in terms of possible experience, for those statements which in their original form are opaque to us.

When first stated this understanding of meaning seemed odd, but now it is difficult to imagine any alternative to it which avoids confusion with psychology but still takes into consideration the sense-experience basis of synthetic propositions. Its seeming oddness, perhaps, lies in the fact that we do not often inquire into the fundamental nature of what makes our sentences meaningful. We learn the methods of verifying the vast majority of our common sentences and the relevant rules of inference at the same time that we learn the language, and—the factual meaning of these sentences thus clear to us—we seldom reflect further about them. "Plainly we all understand, in many cases believe, propositions which we have not in fact taken steps to verify."[8] The philosopher, however, must look beneath the surface of language; and, according to verificational analysis, the results of his investigations tally both with most of our actual unconsidered practice and with the self-conscious techniques of modern scientists.

But there are exceptions to this happy situation. When the verificational analyst exercises his philosophical responsibility to peer under the surface of language, he sometimes finds that the conditions neither for analytic nor for synthetic meaning are present. On these occasions, where language appears to fulfill one of the two functions proper to its essential use but fails to meet the logical requirements of these functions, it is devoid of literal significance and is operating merely on the inherited emotive capital of its component words. "Emotive meaning" in such contexts is parasitical and literally senseless, inasmuch as it fails either to establish linguistic conventions or to allow for any translation into statements about possible experience; and reliance upon emotive meaning alone, where other types are missing, is not so uncommon as might be supposed. A great many speculative thinkers have been in the practice of making assertions which neither are definitions of terms nor offer any possibility of translation into equivalent statements referring to sense-experience. On those occasions, words (all of which individually we understand in other, legitimate, statements) may be arranged in a grammatically correct way but none the less form a sentence which is literally meaningless; for if it is true that the factual meaning of a sentence is identical with the methods of its verification, and if it is discovered that some non-analytic sentences admit no possible method of verification, then we are forced to draw the conclusion that these sentences are literally nonsense, however well disguised they may be to the unsuspecting. The tearing away of the disguises which have too long permitted such nonsense to parade itself as profound significance is, for verificational analysis, one of the prime tasks of philosophical analysis. Let us now look more carefully into the character of these analytical procedures.

III

The philosophical analysis of a putative fact-stating proposition must make explicit what tests of experience would verify a given sentence. From a genuinely meaningful statement a number of possible sense-experiences will be derivable which will be relevant to the verification of the proposition in question.

The word "relevant" is significant. It is true that early in the history of the verification principle extreme claims were made to the effect that fully meaningful sentences must be reducible to possibilities of experience which, with a rule of inference, could *conclusively* verify the proposition under discussion. But verificational analysis soon moved away from this "strong" sense of "verify" to what A. J. Ayer terms the "weak" sense of the word. These philosophers saw that conclusive verification would be out of the question for such vitally important statements as scientific expressions of general law, since no finite set of observations (limited to past experiences) could in principle succeed in verifying *conclusively* a universal statement (dealing with future as well as past observations). The verification principle was admitted in its "weak" form, therefore, with the result that statements admitting the derivation of experience *relevant* to their verification could be held to be meaningful. An important corollary of this modification of the verification principle because of the "open texture"[9] of all empirical language is that synthetic statements may be more or less *probable* (more or less fully verified) but never *necessary* (conclusively verified). To analytic statements alone, therefore, can the adjective "necessary," designating the factually vacuous necessity of linguistic decision, be applied. To synthetic propositions (hence to all discussion of existing things) there attach only greater and lesser degrees of probability.

A variation of the verification principle which we shall meet later is the principle of falsifiability. A positive assertion, obviously, will be logically equivalent to the denial of the negation of itself (for example, the statement "Socrates was a philosopher" is logically equivalent to the statement "It is *not* the case that Socrates was *not* a philosopher"); thus if it is discovered what an assertion denies we are well on the way to discovering what it asserts. The emphasis is shifted from the search for those possible experiences which will verify the statement to the inquiry into the sorts of experience which will falsify (or in some way count against) what has been asserted. This principle of falsifiability or falsification proved particularly useful for dealing with universal law statements; its application to theological discourse, we shall see, has provided much food for thought.

Equipped with these criteria of meaning, verificational analysis is prepared to expose linguistic nonsense masquerading as synthetic propositions. It is in the role of iconoclast and critic, in fact, that philosophical analysis of this sort has become best known to the intellectual world. It has been the task of sweeping away the "rubbish" in language which has captured the imagination and sounded the battle cry of the movement and given it its almost missionary zeal.

The essential procedure is quite simple: confronted with a sentence which seems to assert something to be the case, we search for possible methods of its verification in order to grasp its meaning, but in some cases we can nowhere find—or even conceive of—a sense-experience which might in principle have the slightest relevance to determining the sentence's truth or falsehood. Such a sentence is asserting nothing at all. It cannot be true or false. It is not a genuine proposition but literal nonsense, with which we need not concern ourselves. This is not even idle speculation; it is not speculation at all since the sentences employed fail to convey meaning.

Speculation which is idle, because untestable in practice, as would be the speculation what Socrates ate on his fifth birthday, is now sharply distinguished from pseudo-speculation; in the latter case we are not merely unable to determine the truth or falsity of a thesis, for there is no genuine thesis to be true or false.[10]

Philosophical analysis thus affords us the benefit, verificational analysis concludes, of weeding out sham questions and nonsense from our attention so that we need not waste our time in taking seriously everything that presents itself in a plausible grammatical form.

3

THE "ELIMINATION" OF
THEOLOGICAL DISCOURSE

THE TYPICAL TREATMENT of theological language from the standpoint of verificational analysis is harshly critical. Theological language purports to make assertions about matters of supernatural
fact; but, it is held, in so far as it succeeds in asserting anything at
all it fails to refer beyond natural phenomena. Theological language
claims to state necessary truths; but, it is asserted, it falls instead into
necessary falsehood. Theological language pretends to possess deep
significance; but, it is retorted, at best it can offer only incomprehensibility tinged with emotion.

I

In attempting to defend their claim to some knowledge of the
existence of God, many theists assert that evidence to be found
within "creation"—perhaps the regularity of the cosmic process,
perhaps the experience of visions or mystical intuitions, perhaps the
occurrence of miracles—tends to support their statements about
the supernatural. But all such claims are logically misguided, according to verificational analysis, since no meaningful statement
can in principle be made about "the supernatural." Any statement
which escapes meaninglessness will be discovered to have as its
factual referent only ordinary, natural experiences; and a list of
the protocol-statements reporting these experiences will be equivalent to the whole meaning (other than merely emotive) of the
proposition.

Sometimes theists insist that the statement "God exists" is relevant to a number of actual or possible experiences. "God exists," they claim, entails (for example) the further statement: "seedtime and harvest, cold and heat, summer and winter, day and night, shall not cease" (Genesis 8:22). Such theists are not aware, however, that in this they are in danger of reducing the literal meaning of "God exists" to propositions about weather and agriculture. There is no difficulty in finding experiences which would verify the latter, but the *whole* of what the theist wants to say is quite evidently not expressed in propositions of this kind. A. J. Ayer's classic statement on this subject is as follows:

. . . If the sentence "God exists" entails no more than that certain types of phenomena occur in certain sequences, then to assert the existence of a god will be simply equivalent to asserting that there is the requisite regularity in nature; and no religious man would admit that this was all he intended to assert in asserting the existence of a god.[1]

But what is the "more" which the religious man wishes to assert? If there is to be any factual content to his speech, this content must be expressible in equivalent statements about experience; yet the moment he offers any such experiences it would seem that they would become, for verificational analysis, the *whole* literal meaning of his words. As Thomas McPherson writes concerning the factual meaning of the argument from design, "The deistic hypothesis, as I stated it, runs: There is a supreme orderer who has arranged the universe in an ordered way. The alternative runs, simply: The universe is arranged in an orderly . . . way."[2] So it would seem, inevitably, in every case. Is there any escape from this theological dilemma?

The answer to the problem of maintaining factual content and at the same time supernatural reference for theological language has sometimes been sought by theists in certain unique sorts of experience: mystical intuitions, visions, or miracles. But no escape from the theological impasse is offered even here.

Mystical intuitions, first, fail to provide for meaningful talk about a "supernatural being" both because the statements which are based on such experiences fail to exhibit the characteristics of a factually meaningful statement and because there is no ground for exempting "introspective" experience from the demands on any experience. A meaningful synthetic proposition, as we have seen, is required by verificational analysis to offer the possibility of relevant experience concerning its testing. But the statements which claim factual content on the basis of mystic intuition fail to meet this standard. As Ayer puts it, "We do not deny *a priori* that the mystic is able to discover truths by his own special methods. We wait to hear what are the propositions which embody his discoveries, in order to see whether they are verified or confuted by our empirical observations. But the mystic, so far from producing propositions which are empirically verified, is unable to produce any intelligible propositions at all."[3]

Even if the mystic were able to frame his words in the utmost sobriety, however, verificational analysis could not accept the claim that the factual content of his statements in any way referred to the supernatural. Why should "introspective" experience be thought to be any more "supernatural" than public experience of natural regularities? Alasdair MacIntyre objects that

. . . the point of the experience is allegedly that it conveys information about something other than the experience, namely about the ways of God. Now an experience of a distinctively "mental" kind, a feeling-state or an image cannot of itself yield us any information about anything other than the experience.[4]

Ayer adds ironically,

The theist . . . may believe that his experiences are cognitive experiences, but, unless he can formulate his "knowledge" in propositions that are empirically verifiable, we may be sure that he is deceiving himself. It follows that those philosophers who fill their books with assertions that they intuitively "know" this or that . . . religious "truth" are merely providing material for the psycho-analyst.[5]

Mystic intuition is ruled out, then, as providing factual foundation for theological language. It offers no basis for predictions concerning possible verifying sense-experiences, and it is no more able than is any other kind of experience to support inferences concerning some being beyond all possible experience. Therefore, "in describing his vision the mystic does not give us any information about the external world; he merely gives us indirect information about the condition of his own mind."[6]

Ayer's use of the term "vision" in the above quotation reminds us of a second traditional theistic claim to valid knowledge of the supernatural. What of "visions" which differ from those of the mystic's introspective ecstasy by being apparently sense-perceived or—occasionally—even perceived publicly by an army or a throng of pilgrims? In these cases is not the God beyond all possible experience *inferred* as legitimately as is the far side of the moon from our experiences of this side of the moon, or an invisible fire from perceived smoke?

Again the reply from the logic of verificational analysis is negative. Alasdair MacIntyre admits that superficially an inference from visible phenomena to the invisible facts in the natural realm seems to offer a logical precedent for an inference from religious visions to supernatural realities; but the logical statuses of the two are in fact radically dissimilar. Where we legitimately infer the invisible from the visible it is because we have prior experiential reasons to believe in some connection between the two: we have seen smoke rising from a fire before we infer fire from smoke alone. In the case of religious visions,

. . . in order to infer the divine from an apparition we should have to have experience of a connection between them in the way in which we do have experience of the connection between smoke and fires. But what we experience and all that we experience is the vision, and if indeed we had the additional experience of the divine which we should need in order to assert that it was indeed the author of the vision, we should presumably not require the vision to tell us of the divine.[7]

No sort of correlation of the vision with other observable phenomena would add an ounce of weight to the vision's authority concerning the invisible. Not even amazing predictive power made possible by a vision supposed to reveal God could show that such predictions were actually from *God* and not some other source. A radical division is set between language concerning the observable and that concerning the (in principle) unobservable. "Visions are but one set of phenomena which may or may not be correlated with other phenomena, but they no more than any other occurrence lead us beyond the world of experience."[8]

Inferences from visions, arguments from mystic intuitions, and claims based on very general facts about the world may not provide an experiential base adequate to support meaningful assertions about the supernatural, but can any facts serve more powerfully to undergird the factual significance of theological assertions than *miraculous* events? Here are overt public occurrences, not tarnished with subjectivity, which seem to demand an explanation in terms of the supernatural. And if these events can best be explained by reference to "God," then the claims made for mystic experience, visions, and evidences from nature would appear to be vindicated.

Once again the logic of verificational analysis rules out this suggestion. But not, as may be supposed, by denying *a priori* that miraculous events may have occurred. It is at least logically possible, all must admit, that water may have poured from a rock struck by Moses in the desert, that lepers may have been made clean, that the blind may have been gifted suddenly with sight. These alleged events may properly be called "miracles" simply because if they happened their happening could not adequately be explained in terms of the laws of contemporary scientific theory. But is a supernatural explanation then required, supposing that the report of these events is veridical? There can be no such *logical* requirement. If there were, the "explanation" would become part of the very definition of the event and the theological question would be grossly begged. The explanation for an event must always be kept logically distinct from the report of the occurrence of that event. This being so, we must admit at least the logical possibility of explaining "miracles" as natural occurrences.

But what, more precisely, is meant by a "natural occurrence"? Patrick Nowell-Smith warns us not to confuse the "natural" with what is explainable at any given time by scientific doctrine. Such a definition would be entirely too narrow: it would lead one to the absurd position that many events are "natural" today which were "supernatural" a few years ago and that much that is genuinely "supernatural" today will become entirely "natural" in the future if science continues to progress. The best definition of the "natural," therefore, is a methodological one. On this definition any event is natural if it is open in principle to the scientific *method* of explanation.

To make our concept of the "natural" (and, correspondingly, the "supernatural") more precise, we shall have to digress briefly to examine the logical character of a scientific explanation. But this digression more than anything else may make clear why verificational analysis firmly rejects all attempts to claim "the supernatural" as an explanation for miraculous events—or for any events at all.

Scientific method requires, first, an element of predictability or at least the specification of some experience which might in principle verify or refute the proposed explanation. This requirement safeguards one of the prime characteristics of scientific explanation: its specificity. Verificational analysis provides a logical account of why an explanation, if it is to explain, must explain *some* events and not others: if a theory is open to confirmation by any experience whatsoever, it is saying nothing in particular. But to say nothing in particular is equivalent to saying nothing at all! For this reason all explanations which are logically able to explain—able, that is, to have a definite factual meaning—must be of limited generality. Would-be "explanations" of unlimited generality sacrifice their specificity by flabbily allowing any experience, indiscriminately, to "verify" them. And in so doing they unwittingly sacrifice their power genuinely to explain. Fortunately, scientific method inherently requires this specificity by insisting that some particular experiences be capable in principle of verifying or falsifying any proposed explanation. Even the most wide-ranging explanations of science—the law of gravitation, for example—are far from destroying themselves by pretending to an unlimited generality. "Gravitation accounts for many things, yet not for a fraction of all the things there are."[9]

Second, scientific method requires that a theory, if it is truly to explain, must permit expansibility; that is, application must be found for a would-be explanation beyond the data which originally demanded it. Without a capacity for expansion an alleged "explanation" becomes no more than an *ad hoc* label for a specific phenomenon offered in lieu of a real explanation. Molière was on strong logical ground, therefore, when he ridiculed the seventeenth-century medical profession for allegedly "explaining" events by constructing impressive names for them. To "explain" the phenomenon of sleep by a "dormative agency," or the assimilation of nourishment by "digestive potency"—or, better still, by impressive Latin equivalents—is no more than to disguise ignorance of genuine explanations. An excellent example of an explanation often proved capable of expansibility as well as of predictability and specificity is, once again, the law of gravitation. The reach of the theory which Newton advanced on the basis of relatively few data has expanded vastly beyond the legendary falling apple. It accounts not only for particular falling events on earth but also for the activity of other members of the solar system and the far-off galaxies; it permits experimental confirmation in the laboratory; it allows precise measurements of the gravitational constant. And we have no difficulty in conceiving experiences which would tend to falsify it ("falling" up, and so on), though we know that the actual occurrence of these experiences is immensely improbable.

A third essential characteristic of scientific method is subsumption of the explained phenomenon under a uniformity or, as John Hospers insists, a "law." A true explanation in response to the questions "how" and "why" will not merely show similarities between the familiar and the unfamiliar. This understanding of explanation is both too relativistic and too narrow: too *relativistic* because it would make the validity of an explanation (a logical question) dependent on what happens to be familiar to this person or to that (a psychological question); too *narrow* because it is sometimes the more familiar phenomenon (air pressure in a tire) which requires explanation in terms of the less familiar (the molecular theory of gases), not *vice versa*. Equally unsatisfactory is the demand that explanation—even of the question "why"—always be in terms of purpose. Relative to physical events such purposive explanations either beg the theological question at issue by postulating a divine purpose or relapse into an animism ("The stone sinks in water because it wants to go down") which explains nothing at all ("Why didn't it want to go up?"). With reference to human beings, explanations on the basis of purpose may be to the point, but what makes even such explanations truly explanatory is the implicit subsumption of purposive behavior under a uniformity discovered in the class of purposive beings: *viz.*, when someone has a purpose he normally acts so as to achieve this purpose. If it were not for this familiar uniformity, it would not explain *why* John went to the store merely to assert that it was his purpose to buy ice cream. The subsumption of the act under a uniformity is logically more important than the discovery of purpose, therefore, even in answer to the question "why"; and it is this logical feature of explanation which, together with predictability, specificity, and expansibility, is most typical of scientific explanation.

Now we may return to our original question: must miracles be explained in terms of the supernatural? Patrick Nowell-Smith's answer is forthright: not only is it logically *possible* that miracles be explained as natural events (that is, events open in principle to methods of explanation as reviewed above), but also it is logically *necessary* that they be given a natural explanation if they are to be genuinely explained at all. What, after all, is the theist's own attitude toward alleged miraculous events? First, the theist rejects all right to predictions concerning them; sometimes miracles occur, sometimes not—it is up to "God's inscrutable will" whether or not such events happen. To conduct an experiment with prayer (or to throw oneself down from the pinnacle of the temple to test God's readiness to perform a miracle, as Christ refused to do) is to "tempt God," an impious act which, if followed through unsuccessfully, offers no falsification of theistic claims. Second, the theist shrinks from granting his so-called supernatural "explanation" expansibility. That Peter walked on the water for a time does not have anything to do with the insects which flit over the surface of ponds or with the dynamics of our walking with snowshoes. Third, no subsumption under lawful regularities may be established about miraculous events even on the theist's own view. Those "healed by prayer" do not uniformly gain sudden wealth as well; specified circumstances like dearth of potables at a wedding are not regularly associated with other happenings like water turning into wine. At every point, miracles are carefully excluded (by the theist himself) from the possibility of possessing the characteristics required of a natural explanation. And this is quite understandable. If he failed to do this—if, that is, "miraculous" events were admitted by the theist to be in principle open to following a pattern of predictable uniformity, to offering significant expansibility into other areas of experience, to being subsumed under a law—then the unusual events traditionally called "miracles" would no longer be in principle beyond the scope of natural science. They would instead be odd natural happenings seeking some kind of natural explanations. The theist's firm rejection of predictability, expansibility, and uniformity, therefore, is vital to his position; he is not interested in natural explanations but in his supernatural explanation.

But can the appeal to the "supernatural" even in principle act as an explanation? Manifestly not! A *name* ("supernatural") is being offered for application to these events, but the logical structure which might have made this name more than a tendentious label (in the tradition of "dormative powers") has been carefully evacuated. The "supernatural," as we have repeatedly seen, can, on the logic of verificational analysis, have no factual meaning since no experience of it *per se* is in principle possible and since any experience alleged relevant to it turns out to be inadequate to support any factual significance beyond the experience itself. As an explanation, the "supernatural" offers no basis for specificity. Are miracles relevant experience? So are all natural events, if God sustains the universe. The theistic explanation eliminates itself as a genuine explanation, for verificational analysis, by its claim of unlimited generality as well as by its lack of capacity for expansibility and subsumption. Patrick Nowell-Smith summarizes: "If miracles are 'lawful' it should be possible to state the laws; if not, the alleged explanation amounts to a confession that they are inexplicable."[10]

The analysis of factual meaning which verificational analysis supplies has effectively blocked every attempt at making significant assertions about "the supernatural" or about a transcendent "God." Where the theist claims that he refers to definite experiences, the meaning of his language apparently is wholly exhausted by reference to these experiences—it never "breaks through" to the "beyond." And where the theist is concerned solely with the inexperienceable "beyond," he finds that on the logic of verificational analysis his words are totally empty of factual meaning. It would appear that theological discourse must be judged a failure if its aim is to state anything literally significant about a distinctive supernatural subject matter.

II

A characteristic claim of theists has been that their statements express necessary truths. But verificational analysis is employed to show not only that this claim must be rejected, in so far as the statements of theological discourse purport to state facts about existence, but also that theological language inevitably becomes involved in logical contradiction and thus in necessary falsehood. If this attack can be made to stick, then, it is clear, there is no longer even room for agnosticism (as there might be if the factual emptiness of theological language were its only defect), since a contradiction is not even capable of expressing a logical possibility. Such a situation, J. L. Mackie contends, would mean that the theist "must now be prepared to believe, not merely what cannot be proved, but what can be *disproved* from other beliefs that he also holds."[11]

Mackie chooses the problem of evil as an illustration of the analytic difficulties present within theological discourse. This ancient theological conundrum, Mackie tells us, is essentially a logical problem, consisting in reconciling three equally essential theological statements. It arises only when all three are asserted, yet not to assert all three conjointly is unthinkable for the theist: (1) God is omnipotent, (2) God is wholly good, and (3) evil exists. Mackie's analysis requires three further "quasi-logical rules" connecting the premises: (a) good is opposed to evil, (b) a good thing always eliminates evil as far as it can, and (c) there are no limits (short of the logically impossible) to what an omnipotent being can do. To deny any of the premises, of course, is to escape the problem of evil; that is, to deny the omnipotence of God (impossible for traditional theism), to deny that God is wholly good (still more outrageous to the theologian), or to deny the existence of evil would free the believer from his logical snare. The first two are out of the question for the traditional theist. The third alternative has been tried, but at a price which raises many more problems. Consistently to affirm that there is no such thing as evil, that it is really "good misunderstood" or somehow illusory, releases one from the problem of evil, Mackie insists, only at a cost of cutting the nerve of reality and deadening for the believer the moral seriousness of existence.

As opposed to these possible—but, for the theist, self-defeating —escapes from the logical toils of the problem of evil, there are the various attempts of the theologian to avoid admitting the logical impossibility of his position. In each case, according to Mackie, these prove to be unsatisfactory. "In these, one of the constituent propositions is explicitly rejected, but it is covertly re-asserted or assumed elsewhere in the system."[12]

Mackie distinguishes four primary fallacious pseudo solutions often employed by theistic apologists. First, there is the claim that "good cannot exist without evil" or that "evil is necessary as a counterpart to good." Such an answer is ruled out if God is supposed also to be the author of logical necessity, for if he is Creator of logic then he could have prevented by fiat the presumed logical necessity that "good" could not exist without its logical counterpart (if such it really is). Even if we admit, furthermore, that God's omnipotence may legitimately be limited by logical necessity (as Mackie does), this attempted answer in effect involves a redefinition of "good" so that it is no longer an *absolute quality* characterizing God and opposed by "evil," but only a *relative adjective* gaining its meaning through contrast, just as "great" and "small" cannot exist without each other.

But in this sense greatness is not a quality, not an intrinsic feature of anything; and it would be absurd to think of a movement in favour of greatness and against smallness in this sense. Such a movement would be self-defeating, since relative greatness can be promoted only by a simultaneous promotion of relative smallness. I feel sure that no theists would be content to regard God's goodness as analogous to this—as if what he supports were not the *good* but the *better,* and as if he had the paradoxical aim that all things should be better than other things.[13]

A second attempt at solving the problem of evil is by treating evil so that "evil is necessary as a means to good." Such an answer still more severely restricts God's power; God is not only to be subservient to logical necessity in this case but now to be restricted by causal laws. In sum: "the suggestion that evil is necessary as a means to good solves the problem of evil only by denying one of its constituent propositions, either that God is omnipotent or that 'omnipotent' means what it says."[14]

Third, Mackie finds that some theists hope to defend their logical respectability by the assertion: "the universe is better with some evil in it than it could be if there were no evil." Evil, on this view, makes possible the virtues of sympathy, benevolence, heroism, and the like, which arise only when challenged by evil. Again, evil makes a heightened spiritual sensitivity possible, as in aesthetic contrast, because of the "dissonances" written into the "symphony" of the universe. God's goodness and omnipotence are devoted to maximizing the higher goods (heroism, sympathy, and so on) which emerge thanks to the fact of the lower evils (pain, disease, and the like), provided by God to this end.

Mackie holds that this "solution" fails, however, since there are not only "higher" virtues but also "higher" *vices.* Yet if God were wholly omnipotent and good these "higher" evils (cruelty, callousness, cowardice) would be eliminated by him. If it is answered that "higher evils" are simply challenges to "still higher" goods, then we are on our way into a logically untenable infinite regress, since for every order of good there must be a logically possible evil (its lack or opposite).

Finally, we must turn to the answer made by the theologian to the problem of evil: God supposedly *limits himself* through his desire to grant man a free will. It is better, theists say, that men should be free—and this logically involves that they be able sometimes to err and commit evil—than that men should be merely innocent automata, acting rightly in a wholly determined way. God's omnipotence is self-limiting in the expression of his goodness when he grants the practical possibility of evil in order that the good which man does may be morally worthful and not simply deterministically produced. But, Mackie asks, is the theist's assumption correct that the possibility of evil is a *logically necessary* accompaniment of freedom?

If God has made men such that in their free choices they sometimes prefer what is good and sometimes what is evil, why could he not have made men such that they always freely choose the good?[15]

God *might* have chosen, that is, to make men who would *act freely* but *always rightly*.* "Clearly, his failure to avail himself of this possibility is inconsistent with his being both omnipotent and wholly good."[16]

Even more, if God has given free will to men, does this mean that he *can* not or *will* not prevent evil actions? On the first alternative, he is not omnipotent or "self-limiting" but is externally limited in his power; on the second, he is not combating evil to the limit of his ability. The first alternative is impossible to the theist because of its incompatibility with the omnipotence of God, but the second is ruled out for him because of what, in other contexts, he says about sin; that is, if God is actually doing *better* to allow an evil act to occur (for the sake of freedom) than he would be if he thwarted freedom to prevent sin, then sin and evil are not really the prime opponents of the goodness of God but something else—perhaps "unfreedom."

Such is the dilemma as Mackie portrays it, on which the theist

* For further discussion and criticism of this point see Chap. 9.

finds himself poised by his attempts to retain his language about God at all points without violating what he wants to say about the seriousness of sin and the reality of evil. Quite aside from epistemological issues, Mackie concludes, the theistic position is unable to maintain even its analytic consistency under examination.

Verificational analysis has yet more startling techniques for exhibiting the logically necessary falsity of theological discourse. The logical techniques of this form of analysis no longer leave room for attitudes of "tentative surmise and doubt," according to J. N. Findlay. Not only can verificational analysis show that the language of theism must fail when it sets out to prove the existence of God, but —turning the tables—it can be used to prove conclusively that the existence of such a being is logically impossible.

> For we shall try to show that the Divine Existence can only be conceived, in a religiously satisfactory manner, if we also conceive it as something inescapable and necessary, whether for thought or reality. From which it follows that our modern denial of necessity or rational evidence for such an existence amounts to a demonstration that there cannot be a God.[17]

This logical argument for the non-existence of God here outlined by Findlay consists in two major steps: First, God must be explicitly defined so that the existence of the God of *theism* and not that of the various gods of idolatry is clearly at issue. The God of theism is definable, says Findlay, as the being who is the "adequate object of religious attitudes."[18] What are these attitudes? They are attitudes of total commitment, abasement, deference, and wholehearted devotion. They require, on the part of the theist, that God, to be correspondingly appropriate to such unconditional attitudes, not only must be superior to the worshiper but must exceed men and all other things in a *qualitatively different way,* not in any relative sense of superiority. Any limited being would be out of the question; theism rejects the notion of a finite God as inappropriate or inadequate to the religious attitude.

> And hence we are led on irresistibly to demand that our religious object should have an *unsurpassable* supremacy along all avenues, that it should tower *infinitely* above all other objects.[19]

Such infinite Being must not be one among many but all-comprehensive; it cannot merely happen to exist but must be *necessary* existence.

God mustn't merely cover the territory of the actual, but also, with equal comprehensiveness, the territory of the possible. And not only must the existence of *other* things be unthinkable without him, but his own non-existence must be wholly unthinkable in any circumstances. There must, in short, be no conceivable alternative to an existence properly termed "divine": God must be wholly inescapable, as we remarked previously, whether for thought or reality.[20]

The second step of the argument is to remind ourselves of the logical relation shown by verificational analysis to hold between "necessity" and existence. Wherever language is appropriate to deal with the world of fact, we remember, it does so by means of synthetic propositions. But synthetic propositions never allow for *necessity*, only for greater or less degrees of *probability*. No matter how probable a statement about any fact of existence, it is never beyond our conceiving that it might be proved false by a future experience; but this means that it can never be a necessary statement. *Necessity, safety from all possibility of disproof by experience, we saw to reside only in analytic statements.* But such statements have no dealings with existence; they are only reports of decisions concerning our use of language. "Necessity" and "existence" are logically incompatible notions! Each is legitimate in its own context, just as "round" and "square" are meaningful when properly used; but when combined, the expression "necessary existence" is as absurd as is "round square"!

The religious frame of mind seems, in fact, to be in a quandary; it seems invincibly determined both to eat its cake and have it. It desires the Divine Existence both to have that inescapable character which can, on modern views, only be found where truth reflects an arbitrary convention, and also the character of "making a real difference" which is only possible where truth doesn't have this merely linguistic basis. We may accordingly deny that modern approaches allow us to remain agnostically poised in regard to God: they force us to come down on the atheistic side.[21]

God's "necessary existence" is logically—analytically—required if God, for the believer, is to be truly the God of theism; but this "necessity" is logically impossible. Therefore, Findlay confidently concludes, such a "necessary being" does not exist—or, indeed, even *make sense!*

Theological discourse has utterly failed, according to verificational analysis, in its analytic as well as its synthetic aspect. Far from expressing necessary truths, it becomes ensnared in massive contradictions and in futile attempts to say the logically impossible.

III

The sorry predicament of theological discourse is readily interpreted by the logic of verificational analysis. Factual meaning is lacking for theological statements because of theism's inherent violation of the requirement that all synthetic propositions be open, in principle, to verification or falsification by experience. And the logical contradictions within theological speech arise from the misguided attempt to discuss a pseudo subject matter which inevitably leads all who will follow into paradox and incomprehensibility. The cause for this theological misuse of language is to be found in the emotions—for emotive meaning is the only "meaning" which theological discourse may claim.

Antony Flew diagnoses the source of the logical malady which, according to verificational analysis, undermines the entire language of theism. This source, according to Flew, is the *unfalsifiability* of theological statements. To illustrate his position Flew paraphrases a parable told originally by Professor John Wisdom:

Once upon a time two explorers came upon a clearing in the jungle. In the clearing were growing many flowers and many weeds. One explorer says, "Some gardener must tend this plot." The other disagrees, "There is no gardener." So they pitch their tents and set a watch. No gardener is ever seen. "But perhaps he is an invisible gardener." So they set up a barbed-wire fence. They electrify it. They patrol it with bloodhounds. (For they remember how H. G. Wells's *The Invisible Man* could be both smelt and touched though he could not be seen.) But no shrieks ever suggest that some intruder has received a shock. No movements of the wire ever betray an invisible climber. The bloodhounds never give cry. Yet still the Believer is not convinced. "But there is a gardener, invisible, intangible, insensible to electric shocks, a gardener who has no scent and makes no sound, a gardener who comes secretly to look after the garden which he loves." At last the Sceptic despairs, "But what remains of your original assertion? Just how does what you call an invisible, intangible, eternally elusive gardener differ from an imaginary gardener or even from no gardener at all?"[22]

Such a story illustrates the manner in which language may initially assert something quite definite but end, after a slow series of retreats from falsification, by saying nothing at all. "Someone may dissipate his assertion completely without noticing that he has done so. A fine brash hypothesis may thus be killed by inches, the death by a thousand qualifications."[23] If the meaning of a statement is identical with the experiences relevant to its verification (or what is logically closely connected, as we noticed earlier—its falsification), then gradually to remove an assertion from the possibility of verification or falsification is, in effect, gradually to strip this language of its meaning. Its friends, in their anxiety to prevent it from being proved false, have turned its worst enemy by transforming it from vulnerable meaningfulness to secure vacuity!

"And in this, it seems to me, lies the peculiar danger, the endemic evil, of theological utterance."[24] In earlier days prophets might castigate their sinning compatriots by announcing that a flood or a crop failure was God's act of punishment for wickedness. As better natural explanations for such natural events have become available, however, theistic language has retreated from the possibility of falsification, no longer promising natural disasters to follow in the wake of moral disorders. At any point where fact might tell against the language of theology, theological speech is hastily qualified to keep it from falsification. This process of retreat from verification has continued to such a point that

. . . now it often seems to people who are not religious as if there was no conceivable event or series of events the occurrence of which would be admitted by sophisticated religious people to be a sufficient reason for conceding "There wasn't a God after all" or "God does not really love us then."[25]

When *any* state of events is compatible with an assertion, then the putative assertion is either analytic or meaningless.

Someone tells us that God loves us as a father loves his children. We are reassured. But then we see a child dying of inoperable cancer of the throat. His earthly father is driven frantic in his efforts to help, but his Heavenly Father reveals no obvious sign of concern. Some qualification is made—God's love is "not a merely human love" or it is "an inscrutable love," perhaps—and we realize that such sufferings are quite compatible with the truth of the assertion that "God loves us as a father (but, of course, . . .)." We are reassured again. But then perhaps we ask: what is this assurance of God's (appropriately qualified) love worth, what is this apparent guarantee really a guarantee against? Just what would have to happen not merely (morally and wrongly) to tempt but also (logically and rightly) to entitle us to say "God does not love us" or even "God does not exist"?[26]

Until this question is answered, Flew contends, the theist's language is doomed by its slippery compatibility with every state of affairs to be empty of factual meaning; but once the theist ventures to answer, his language has been opened to falsification and thus to probable disproof.

The factual vacuity which verificational analysis discovers to be intrinsic to theological discourse is combined, as we have seen, with an analytically contradictory character. The cause for this inevitable failure in logical consistency is traced by Bernard Williams to the nature of the supposed subject matter of theological speech. At root theological language is, as we have seen, "words-about-God"; but any such language will be destined to fall into "a sort of inherent and necessary incomprehensibility,"[27] according to Williams, because at some point a *relation* of some kind must be postulated between supernatural God and natural world. Perhaps the relation will be taken to be the Incarnation, as in Christian doctrine; perhaps, more generally, the relation will be attempted merely by human words purporting to speak about "God." But precisely here lies the rub:

The statement of these relations will be itself unsatisfactory, and will involve others that are so: because the concepts required—of fatherhood, for instance, and of love, and of power—are acquired in a human context; the language of these things is a language that grows and is used for the relations of humans to humans. To say that, while this is so, religious language requires merely an extrapolation from the human context, is not to solve the problem but to pose it again. For the extrapolation required is an extrapolation to infinity, and in even trying to give a sense to this we encounter the incomprehensibility.[28]

This incomprehensibility is often excused—even welcomed—by theists on the ground that it "leaves room for faith." Kierkegaard and his modern followers glory in the "supreme absurdity" that the infinite could have anything to do with the finite. Such an attempted answer cannot satisfy, however, since faith must be *in* something. To be asked to have faith despite logical difficulties may be a sufficiently strange request:

But it is a stranger request to ask someone by faith to believe something that he does not properly understand; for what is it that he is being asked to believe? Faith might be a way of believing something, as opposed to believing it on evidences; but how could it be a way of stepping from what is understood to what is not understood?[29]

The religious person must, on this analysis, seriously consider the question "If you do not know what it is you are believing on faith, how can you be sure that you are believing anything?"[30] What is the difference between "believing" something incomprehensible and "disbelieving" it? One cannot *believe* that "boojums are inflabulated," but one cannot *disbelieve* it either. One's only logically appropriate stand when confronted with incomprehensibility is a demand for clarification; "belief," even with the best of good will, must wait upon the provision of a content to believe. Thus religious evasion—even through "blind belief"—of the difficulties met by theological discourse in offering meaningful content is ruled out. "Blind belief" in this case is logically equivalent to "blind unbelief"; both are sure to err.

The combined weight of argument from the perspective of verificational analysis in criticism of theological discourse convinces Thomas McPherson, among many others, that the total elimination of this language has been effected. "The things that theologians try to say (or some of them) belong to the class of things that just cannot be said."[31] The discovery, as McPherson believes, of basic logical maladies within theological language may be the source of profound "worry" to theists; but for this he offers a remedy. "The way out of the worry is retreat into silence."[32] This is a startling suggestion, perhaps; it involves the suicide of systematic theology and the end of all religious talk. But such an outcome should not be of too great discouragement, McPherson says, to the theist who cares more for worship than for words. In support of this point he reminds us of Rudolf Otto's insight that the really important elements in religion are the aspects of faith which cannot be conceptualized. In destroying theological language verificational analysis has aided the truly religious person by preventing the temptation to seek God in the wrong places. McPherson insists that

. . . a branding of religious assertions as "nonsense" need not be anti-religious. It can be interpreted as an attack on those who in the name of religion are perverting religion. It can be interpreted as a return to the truth about religion. Otto conceived himself in *The Idea of the Holy* to be recovering the essential element in religion—which had been in danger of being lost under a cloud of rationalizing. What is essential about religion is its non-rational side, the part that cannot be . . . put into words.[33]

McPherson, as we have seen, hopes to soften the blow which he is convinced has fallen irrevocably upon theological language by arguing that this fatal thrust from verificational analysis can be of concern only to a few—or, at least, only to those halfhearted believers who value speech above the sacred.

But is this argument justified? It seems to me that theists must at last face the issue bluntly: to abandon the right to use theological language is to abandon what many besides professional "religionists" take to be the most important aspects of their religion. First, the loss of language would be equivalent to the loss of all cognitive claims for religion; no longer could the religious person hope to know or even believe religious "truths." There could be no such thing as religious "truths" since these abstract concepts could never be formulated by a religion without a language. Second, what would become of public worship without language? Public worship requires at the very least the focusing of attention on common concepts, shared and openly acknowledged by the group. Even this would be forfeit; still more obviously casualties of the loss of language would be all hymns, verbal prayer, and preaching. Third, no telling to one another of the "good news" of one's religion would be possible without language. All attempts at religious conversation and conversion would cease, and therefore all missionary activity would need to halt. With no function in public worship or in missions, organized religion would be radically changed in character and probably gradually "wither away." Fourth, even "private religion" would need radically to be altered, for no belief could be entertained, even privately, without the vehicle for its formulation. Private prayer, made wordless, would become no more than vague and amorphous feeling-states; no longer could one even find religious renewal in contemplating one's most profound convictions. The importance of language for all thought may sometimes be exaggerated, as, for example, H. H. Price skillfully argues in *Thinking and Experience,* but its importance for higher thought, for abstract thought, for disciplined thought—for distinctly human thought—cannot be overstated. Abandoning language would be tantamount to dismissing religion as an important human activity and substituting, not the mystic's high ecstasy forged in discipline, contemplation, and study, but the formless "rosy glow" of "positive thinking"—without even the thought to think positively!

These are some of the consequences which, I believe, would follow a real loss of theological discourse. Many would applaud and consider these consequences desirable; many more would be profoundly disturbed by them. But whether we are elated or depressed —or indifferent—has little bearing at this point. A powerful philosophical attack has been launched, and it will not strengthen or refute it to cheer or to deplore the effects it may have on cherished beliefs and institutions.

IV

Before we proceed to examine critically the foregoing arguments against theological discourse in particular and the logical foundations of verificational analysis in general, we should stop to consider whether theological speech may not be accommodated, somehow, to the logic of verificational analysis.

David Cox, in an article in *Mind,* recommends the verification principle of meaning to theologians, on condition that one revision be accepted in its formulation: the requirement that some *sense*-experience be relevant to any meaningful non-tautological statement must be modified to allow that "an ostensible statement of fact is significant if, and only if, it can, in principle, be verified by human experience."[34] Once we accept this version of the verification principle, admitting more kinds of experience than sense-experience to be capable of verifying a proposition, the threat presented by verificational analysis to theological discourse is removed, Cox believes. Theologians should then no longer hesitate to accept the classification of their language into either analytic rules, on the one hand, "that is, statements which indicate in what ways the terms of theological jargon are to be used,"[35] or empirical hypotheses, on the other hand, "that is, significant statements which can be verified by human experience."[36]

Such acceptance would involve certain sacrifices on the part of the theologian, Cox admits (such as the readiness to "accept the possibility that some doctrines may be non-significant" and the willingness to hold their doctrines as "always, in principle, liable to modification, or contradiction by subsequent experience"), but these drawbacks would be more than balanced by the advantages which would accrue. The advantages would be threefold: first, the apologetic position of theology would be immeasurably strengthened. Theological language, securely rooted in human experience, would no longer be vulnerable to the hostility of verificational analysis. The most radical voices of criticism would be silenced. Second, theological doctrine would be brought once again into relevance to human life and ordinary experience; theistic language would no longer be open to the accusation of being out of touch with daily existence. And third, the language of contemporary Christians would be brought back into the service of the same function for which the earliest formulators of theological doctrine used theirs: to safeguard Christian experience.

> Originally Christian doctrine was not intended to provide a description of what might be called "transcendent reality." . . . In textbooks and in lectures it is asserted that the Christian church was compelled to formulate her doctrines in order to "safeguard Christian experience." . . . So long as doctrines are no more than is sufficient for the purpose of safeguarding experience they will be significant by the test of the verification principle.[37]

Thus verificational analysis, employing an anti-metaphysical weapon forged by the early logical positivists, forces the theologian willy-nilly to return, Cox insists, to the practices of the early Church. This reformation of theology may come from without, but it is a reformation to be welcomed.

As examples of the amenability of theistic language to analysis in terms of possible verifying experience Cox offers us two restatements of traditional doctrine in what he considers readily significant form. First, "God exists" may be treated in the following manner: the rules governing the use of "God" will initially be given, stressing that the word is not "rightly to be used except in such phrases as 'meeting God,' or 'encountering God,' or 'knowing God' ";[38] then the empirical hypothesis, reflecting the fact that many human beings have had experiences which are like "personal encounter" but lacking the sense-experiences usually associated with such encounter, may be stated: "Some men and women have had, and all may have, experiences called 'meeting God.' "[39] In this restatement lies all the empirical significance of the theistic claim that "God exists"; more is superfluous.

The second possible example of doctrinal restatement, "God created the world from nothing," connects human experience of "meeting God" with daily experiences of the world around us. Its original purpose was "to assert that the world is God's world, and that nothing in it is opposed to Him if it is properly used."[40]

Now if we assert that the experience called "meeting God" can be regarded as the encounter with a person who has a concern for the well-being of men, then we can state the doctrine "God created the world from nothing" "everything which we call 'material' can be used in such a way that it contributes to the well-being of men."[41]

Such restatements of theological language as these are only preliminary examples of what a theology may be able to achieve, Cox holds, once it learns its painful lesson from verificational analysis. It is true that all the empirical hypotheses of the theologians would be verifiable only "in principle" since the methods of verification must involve a high degree of risk, subjectivity, patience, and uncertainty ("If they don't come off, the experimenter can never be quite sure that it was not his fault"[42]), but the job of restatement is urgently important in today's intellectual climate. To refuse is to place oneself in an almost impossible position. "Those who wish to retain doctrines which cannot be stated in a verifiable form have to explain in what sense they 'understand' such doctrines."[43]

I cannot avoid coming to the conclusion, however, that Cox's article, as one of the most thoughtful recent attempts to accommodate theism to verificational analysis, merely illustrates the more vividly the radical incompatibility which holds between this movement of modern philosophy and traditional theism. Criticisms of Cox's point of view may be launched from two sides, first the philosophical and then the theological.

From the position of verificational analysis it is difficult to understand how anything short of intersubjective phenomena can succeed in "verifying" a putative proposition. The emphasis on sense-experience is not without much justification, and it most definitely does not entail a behavioristic position in which the occurrence of non-sensory experiences must be denied, as Cox at one point seems to allege. Even A. J. Ayer, in *Language, Truth and Logic,* where one of the most thoroughgoing early statements of the verification principle of meaning was propounded, both recognizes the fact of memory images (which are not themselves sense-contents but merely "correspond to sense-contents") and deals with other "mental states" in terms of "introspective" sense-contents (which, by the way, seems to indicate a somewhat elastic use of the term "sense"). Gilbert Ryle's *Concept of Mind* aside, there has been little sustained effort to bring into question the actuality of "human experience" other than sense-experience of the physical world—and even Ryle's quasi-behaviorist approach to this issue has puzzled many philosophical interpreters as to precisely how its denials are to be understood. No, the rejection of any but sense-experience for purposes of verification must not be taken as equivalent to the assertion of the highly improbable hypothesis that human experience is exhausted by sense-experience. On the contrary, its purpose is to safeguard the objectivity of empirical truth. If individual, unconfirmable experience be taken as "verifying" some propositions, what is to be taken as verifying, in turn, the truth of statements about these "private" experiences? No experience, "public" or "private," would be relevant for such a task, and the very quest for verification itself would lead to a morass of meaninglessness. Again, what is to prevent all manner of subjective delusion from masquerading as "verifying" experience? The insistence on sense-experience and the quest for objectivity and dependable truths are one and the same.

It is on this basis that a rebuttal to Cox published in *Mind* by Thomas McPherson must be understood. McPherson argues that the verb "to meet" essentially involves certain sense-experience correlations which must in principle be lacking in Cox's example of "meeting God." Nor is the problem peculiar to the verb "to meet"; "The trouble is that statements using words like 'meet' are all verifiable, but only in the way Mr. Cox does not want, *i.e.* they are verifiable by *sense* experience."[44] Cox merely shows that he misunderstands the basic thrust of McPherson's point when he answers that we say that people can "meet" over the telephone without actually being in physical presence of one another.[45] Telephone conversations (Cox seems to forget) are public events which are always open in principle to intersubjective (sense) confirmation.

Theologically, Cox's attempt to reconcile verificational analysis and theism fares no better. Cox has claimed that the whole meaning of "God exists" is adequately rendered in terms of human experiences of a certain kind which are defined as "meeting God." We meaningfully assert, however, that many things existed before any men were on the scene to experience them; shall we say of God that his existence is somehow more dependent on human "meeting-experience" than are geological strata? But then, asks McPherson precisely to the point, "did God not exist at all before men existed?"[46] When theists say "God exists" they are not, despite Cox, referring in a veiled way to experience alone. They suppose themselves talking of an independently real Being whose existence is independent of any human wish or feeling-state. What the existence of God means to the theist cannot be reduced, without residue, to experiential terms. As W. D. Glasgow concludes,

> Mr Cox would maintain that the essential content of the doctrine is unaffected by his reformulation. This I wish to deny. Logical positivism and theism are incompatible, and when one is applied to the other, the metaphysical element, that is an integral part of theism, is lost.[47]

Cox's argument supposedly helping theology to understand itself in fact misunderstands an essential element of the religious perspective. No number of linguistic rules licensing the speaker to use "God" language about certain of his experiences will substitute for a belief in a Being existing and active independent of human experience and human definitions. As it stands, this argument is a form of naturalism permitting itself to utilize religious phrases. Cox's belief serves us, unintentionally, as a vivid reminder of the unbridgeable gap that yawns between traditional theism and verificational analysis.

4

THE LIMITS OF
VERIFICATIONAL ANALYSIS

THE PHILOSOPHICAL position we are examining has much to commend it. It is forthright, pellucid, and uncompromising on its principles. But these principles are open to serious philosophical criticisms which tend to impose limits on the effectiveness of verificational analysis as an independent or self-sufficient philosophical position. The individual arguments, too, outlined in the preceding chapter, are vulnerable to attack at many points. It would be tempting to devote much attention to these individual weaknesses, but the relatively non-technical approach adopted for this book rules out counter-analyses of great detail. Instead, let us survey the general boundaries of verificational analysis—boundaries which, unfortunately, verificational analysts often fail to notice.

I

One of the limitations of verificational analysis which is least recognized (perhaps because it is so uniformly pervasive) is to be found in its concept of "fact." Considering the enormous stress placed on "factual significance" by this philosophical position, it is surprising that a more self-conscious analysis of the various possible uses of the word "fact" has not been more characteristic of verificational analysis.

One may speak, without violating the ordinary uses of language, of mathematical "facts," "facts" of logic—even moral "facts"—as well as empirical "facts."* But verificational analysis narrows the

---

* We shall return to a discussion of these points in Chap. 12.

meaning of "fact" and "factual" to contexts relevant to our empirical vocabulary alone. The right of any individual or group to provide narrow technical definitions for words which, in common use, are often so vague as to be useless is not questioned; but this process, when it is employed, must be self-conscious and explicit for all to see. The explicitness is particularly vital when, as in the case of "fact," the word in question is invested with powerful emotional content. A failure to follow this rule makes of the resulting definition a "persuasive definition,"[1] one which achieves its ends more by subtle suggestion than by honest argument.

And it is clear that verificational analysis is covertly urging an evaluation as well as employing a term in a technical manner when it limits the application of "factual" to the class of statements relevant to actual or possible sense-experience. "Facts" are important, we feel; and what has no "factual" significance cannot be of great interest. Thus if the statements of the moralist or the theologian have no "factual" content, they are hardly fit for serious consideration. But such a use of the term "factual" may be tendentious. Perhaps the claim has never been that the reference of such language is to *this kind of* fact. Then, unless it can somehow be *shown* (not merely assumed) that empirical facts are the only kind of facts, the inability of theological assertions to refer to empirical facts is not *ipso facto* to dismiss them as useless or unimportant or totally non-significant.

Ayer is quite correct when he says of the language of the mystic that it "does not give us any information about the external world." The religious person, when he talks about "God," is not merely speaking in a disguised way about the world. So much is made abundantly clear by verificational analysis, and theists who suppose that their speech is somehow like scientific language will do well to learn, once and for all, this lesson. But few theists are in danger of making this mistake. As Ayer himself recognizes, the essential purpose of theological language is to speak about something "more," beyond the "external world," the description of the latter being rightly left to the empirical sciences. There remain many problems confronting language which hopes to speak meaningfully about supernatural "facts," as we shall see below, but we shall not advance our understanding of theological language by making it analytically impossible—as does verificational analysis—for language to refer to any but scientific facts. Such victories are too cheap to be convincing.

A similar narrowness of definition is discoverable in the treatment of "explanation" supplied by verificational analysis. Here, it must be acknowledged, there seems to be considerable justification for attacking at length the theist's common assumption that his "explanations" function with a logic that is on the same order as—or in conflict with—scientific explanations. History is full of disputes between science and religion based on this mistake—a mistake shared both by defenders of religion when they attacked scientific explanation for theological purposes and by defenders of science when they scoffed at religious belief on scientific grounds. But in so far as such conflicts have raged, a failure to distinguish the logical character of scientific from theological explanations has been at fault. Many theists of our own day need to listen to the analyses of Nowell-Smith and Hospers in order to divest themselves of the notion that their theological "explanations" are capable in principle of functioning in the same way as those of the scientist. Language which is used to argue with scientists on scientific matters may have the sound and vocabulary of theological language, but it does not share its logic; it ceases in such contexts to be theological language only to become inferior scientific speech.

But if we acknowledge the fact (a *logical* fact!) that language about a supernatural God cannot function adequately as a scientific explanation and that many theists in past and present are mistaken in supposing that it can, we need not also hold that the only legitimate definition of "explanation" must be in terms of the methods of scientific explanation. One may, if he likes, take the position that only those theories which possess the logical characteristics of a scientific method (prediction, specificity, expansion, and subsumption) are worthy of the honorific title "explanation." This, as a verbal decision, would have much to recommend it. It does not, however, settle the question as to whether or not there are other rational methods of providing ourselves with the kind of coherent theoretical orientation and practical confidence which, on another view, would be taken as the defining characteristics of a wider class of "explanations," scientific or non-scientific. Perhaps there might be a point to making a verbal distinction between the class of scientific explanations (explanations-A) and the class of all other kinds of explanations (explanations-B) which serve similar functions without employing the same logical criteria. Metaphysical explanations-B, for example, may stress synoptic inclusiveness, the logical and psychological drive for "coherence," as James puts it,[2] to an extent which the more specific—and more demonstrably reliable—explanatory techniques of science cannot match. Would such explanations-B necessarily abandon all rational (including empirical) criteria? It would seem not necessary in principle for them to do so. One might ask of any explanation-B how much of our experience of all kinds it takes into account, how much evidence it ignores or distorts, how fully and how naturally it may be related to explanations-A and to other explanations-B, how logically consistent it is within itself, how coherently its principles support one another, and so on.[*]

It may, in the last resort, be found of either type of explanation that its value depends on what one wants to *do* with it. If someone from the tropics asks me to explain the freezing of water (in order to avoid expensive automobile repairs), it will be little help if I deliver a lecture to him on systematic theology. But if one is interested in a different sphere of human activity, perhaps in ordering one's life intelligently in choosing ultimate personal and social goals, an explanation-A dealing with the nature of the empirical universe in terms of some scientific formula (no matter how open to prediction, expansion, and subsumption) will not be logically appropriate.

Now the question becomes: is the essential manner in which theological language offers "explanation" to be understood as explanation-A or as some kind of explanation-B? That theological discourse has been shown to be untenable when interpreted as pseudo-scientific explanation does not, it would appear, rule out the possibility of its functioning rationally and legitimately in some other way. Verificational analysis does not recognize any other way, but this may illustrate a shortcoming more in verificational analysis than in theological language.

II

Verificational analysis exhibits its own narrowness when dealing with theological language in its capacity of communicating factual

* Further attention to these suggestions will be given in Chap. 12.

significance—in some sense, not yet discussed, of "factual"—and in its role of providing "explanations" in some non-scientific sense of "explanation." A similar narrowness becomes evident when we reflect on the position taken by verificational analysis concerning the allegedly "necessarily false" statements of theological discourse. Paradox is equated with sheer contradiction, and the least sympathetic interpretation is put on traditional terminology.

Paradox is no doubt frequently no more than a euphemism for contradiction, but this need not always be the case, as John Wisdom among other contemporary philosophers is quick to point out. Sometimes paradox may be philosophically useful or cognitively illuminating; but verificational analysis fails to notice this fact. In this failure much of the rigidity of verificational analysis is epitomized, and much of the source of this philosophical position's insensitivity to the flexibility of creative new uses of language is revealed. Examine the history of philosophy, Wisdom urges, and you will find that philosophers of great insight seem determined none the less to make contradictory statements. Strangely enough,

. . . these untruths persist. This is not merely because they are symptoms of an intractable disorder but because they are philosophically useful. The curious thing is that their philosophical usefulness depends upon their paradoxicalness and thus upon their falsehood. They are false because they are needed where ordinary language fails. . . .[3]

Wisdom, in contrast to the antiseptic demands of verificational analysis, which treats paradoxes as symptoms of mere linguistic confusion, says: "I wish to represent them as also symptoms of linguistic penetration."[4] The best way to understand a paradox is to take it seriously, not to dismiss it scornfully without examination.

Often we don't properly understand a paradox until, beginning by regarding it literally, we have noted objections to it and held to it because of the reasons for it, and again noted objections and again held to it, and have come by this route to a state where we are no longer driven to assert it or to deny it.[5]

If we consent to attempt this subtler form of analysis we may discover, as verificational analysis is not equipped to discover, that theological paradoxes, like those pointed out by J. L. Mackie, may be the stimulating occasion for more profound theological formulation and richer valuational awareness. Theological paradoxes may be goads to continuing thought and refinement of terminology, somewhat as the so-called "paradoxes of material implication" have been fruitful stimuli in logical theory toward a more precise understanding of the nature of implication.

Mackie has drawn out a few theological paradoxes for our inspection, but he has stopped at what, on this view, would be the beginning of the creative analysis of theological discourse. He has shown, for example, that paradoxes flow from the problem of evil in conjunction with the quasi-logical rule that good is opposed to evil. But he has not gone on, prompted by the paradox, to ask more precisely what is understood by "good" and "evil" in the context of theological discourse. The quasi-logical rule, here, is so platitudinous as to be almost hopelessly vague; he has not stopped to ask whether its very vagueness may not be the true source of the paradox. "Evil," from a theistic point of view, is not necessarily applicable to anything which to the man on the street may seem evil. "Good," likewise, cannot be assumed to be opposed to all that, from any point of view, may appear evil. This is *not* to deny that the words "good" and "evil" have a reliably ascertainable meaning (theologians who claim that human beings cannot know what "good" really means do themselves a disservice, deny all possibility for moral exhortation, and gratuitously undermine the meaningfulness of scriptural codes of ethics), but it is to claim that within the context of theological discourse it is not always possible to know the *denotation* (the actual things referred to by the term) of "good" and "evil," although the *designation* (abstract meaning or defining characteristics) of these words be ever so clear. It is always too easy to assume that one knows what *things* are good and what *events* are evil as God evaluates them; but the absolute point of view, the only point of view from which the platitude "good is always opposed to evil" makes sense, is not available to men. A good God will always be opposed to evil, but only to what is *really* evil. This analysis of the meaning of "good" in theological language is not without relevance to experience. Far from being an empty scholastic exercise in redefinition, it may have a great bearing on one's moral experience if one is forced, in the light of theological definition, to reconsider and perhaps to re-evaluate what are the most fundamental evils (and goods) of human life.

One's moral sensitivity may be enhanced, for example, by a recognition that pleasure may not in every case be "good," or pain and sickness always "evil" in the theological vocabulary.

A similar analysis of the theological use of the words "power" and "freedom" could be offered with respect to the second and third of Mackie's quasi-logical rules, but the style in which the more tolerant—and more fruitful—type of philosophical analysis would be carried on has been sufficiently indicated. Verificational analysis finds nothing in a paradox but logical contradiction and unmeaning, but a fuller philosophical analysis will not be satisfied to stop with this. Verificational analysis is not equipped to recognize any procedure for penetrating behind a paradox. In this fact we find another of its limitations.

A further confining characteristic which tends to be associated with the application of the logic of verificational analysis is the readiness of many philosophers to place a narrow or unsympathetic interpretation on the traditional terminology of theology, seeking to force words which were coined in earlier centuries into the contemporary technical vocabulary—and expressing shocked surprise at the resulting logical confusion!

It is this error which is manifested in Findlay's influential attempt to show the logical impossibility of the existence of God as a "necessary existent." But before I turn to this error in more detail it is only fair that I defend Findlay against a charge often heard in religious circles: that is, that Findlay's is only the "ontological argument" in reverse and, as such, that it suffers from the same defects which have been recognized for centuries in that argument. On the "modern view" on which Findlay bases his analysis (these critics point out), logical necessities do not legislate for matters of fact. How can an argument claiming the necessity of logic (which is analytic) make a claim about the existence or non-existence of God (which claim would be synthetic)? Does it make sense for Findlay to talk about the logical necessity of the non-existence of God?

To this objection I believe that Findlay has a valid reply. His argument, he might say, is intended to show that the true logic of the word "God" is such that the issue of existence cannot even be *raised* about its referent. As in the case of "four-sided triangles," there can be no concept—no meaningful referent which might or might not exist—since analytic rules for the correct employment of "necessary" and "existence" prevent the formulation of any non-contradictory concept.

On the other hand, Findlay may be tellingly criticized for basing his argument on a confusion of two senses of the word "necessary," and (surprisingly enough) for falling into a variant of the same error of which he accuses the theist. The meaning of "necessary" when applied metaphysically to God must, if one is to be historically fair, be distinguished from the meaning of "necessary" when one is dealing, in terms of modern logic, with propositions.

The necessity of God's existence is not the same as the necessity of a logical implication. It means, for those who believe in it, God's complete actuality, indestructibility, *aseitas* or independence of limiting conditions. It is a property ascribed to God, not a property of our assertions about God.[6]

Findlay has leaped prematurely to the conclusion that the ancient theological employment of the word is identical with the modern logical one. Had he been more attentive to the actual employment of the word in the theological context, he would not have fallen into this mistake. If Findlay objects that the word "necessary" ought now to be used only in the context of logic, we might agree; but then the theological discussion would have to be carried on in quite explicitly different terminology, and Findlay's strictures against theological discourse for misusing "necessity" would no longer be required. Findlay's argument, it appears, relies on a confusion between two meanings of an ambiguous term; if the confusion is dispelled so that the theologians are careful to use ontological terms ("aseitas") rather than logical ones ("necessity"), his argument will be seen to be beside the point.

But Findlay, further, has himself fallen into a subtle error of the very sort he condemns when he suggests that his argument showing the logical impossibility of conjoining the words "necessary" and "existence" has the effect of proving that all existence must be merely contingent, thus ruling out an existent God who is at the same time the appropriate object of religious attitudes. "Existence" cannot be modified by the *logical* adjective "necessary," it is true; but by the same token neither can "existence" be said to be merely "contingent"! *Contingency, like necessity, is logically*

appropriate to propositions alone. To discover that "necessary existence" is devoid of meaning is not to make a basic discovery
about the nature of reality—that it must be "contingent" (which,
of course, means nothing on the modern use of the word)—but is
only to be reminded that existent realities are whatever they are,
perishable or self-sustaining, without the by-your-leave of logic.
Perhaps Findlay has at this point come to share, after all, the illusion underlying the ontological argument that something about the
nature of reality can be determined from pure logic. But those who
are acquainted with the thoroughly analytic nature of logic will see
that the factual question as to whether or not there is in reality a
being which is the sufficient cause for its own existence cannot in
principle be settled by Findlay's purely deductive techniques.

Verificational analysis may be seen to have logical limits both
in its treatment of factual assertions and explanations and in its
approach to the analytic aspects of language. Theological discourse
is by no means vindicated in the discovery of these limitations, but
we may at least be assured that it has not so easily been eliminated
by the logic of verificational analysis as many in our time have
supposed.

III

What in the theories of meaning and language held by verificational analysis accounts for the limits we have noted in its scope
and effectiveness? The very diagnosis which this position offers
concerning the ills of theological discourse in general suggests an
answer.

Theological statements, verificational analysis complains, are not
empirically falsifiable; consequently they are devoid of meaning.
Antony Flew's challenge to theists, that they either specify what
occurrences would falsify their claims or admit that they are making no claims at all, has provoked a good deal of worth-while discussion among defenders of theological language. If one accepts
Flew's premise that the meaning of an assertion must always be
equivalent to the perceptible events relevant to its verification or
falsification, then several logical alternatives—each with its cham-
pions—are open to theists. These alternatives are the following:
one may assert that theological statements are relevant to falsification but never conclusively falsifiable; one may hold that they are

wholly unfalsifiable because they are not assertions at all; one may take the view that they are assertions which can be falsified in principle and in practice; or one may claim that they are falsifiable in principle but not in practice.

Basil Mitchell chooses the first approach. The problem of evil, he points out, is a problem to theists precisely because some events tend to falsify theological assertions. But the attitude of the religious person will ultimately prevent anything from counting *decisively* against his beliefs. The scientific observer may be willing to shrug and conclude that he was wrong about his empirical hypotheses, but the very nature of faith precludes the taking of theological assertions as merely "provisional hypotheses to be discarded if experience tells against them."[7]

The consequence of this view, of course, is that any abandonment of religious belief will not be on the basis of evidence but will in every case be due to a "failure of faith." At no point can a line be drawn beyond which faith becomes "irrational" or even insane. R. M. Hare, accepting this implication, admits that theological statements share the logic of utterances made by a lunatic —but he mitigates this admission by insisting that we all must rely on such utterances, which he calls *"bliks."* If someone were to believe with pathological intensity that all Oxford dons were secretly planning to murder him, he could be dissuaded from such a view by no finite number of demonstrations that the dons were really entirely inoffensive. His *blik* prevents his accepting the possibility that any proofs might be capable of falsifying his governing idea. Theological language shares this logic. Thus Flew is right, according to Hare, in denying that anything is asserted by it; but he is wrong in supposing that a *blik* should function as an assertion does. Normal *bliks,* like the unalterable belief of most persons that things will continue to happen regularly in the future as they have in the past, are psychological presuppositions for all our theory and practice. As such, theological statements are in august company, for it is false to suppose that because our *bliks* are not assertions it is unimportant which *bliks* we have. "Flew has shown that a *blik* does not consist in an assertion or system of them; but nevertheless it is very important to have the right *blik.*"[8]

Hare's view invokes its opposite. Many theists may be entirely unwilling to agree that they are asserting nothing empirically defi-

nite when they say "God will take care of you," or "God will
continue to give his Holy Spirit to the Church." What of the biblical promises to the effect that a life lived genuinely in accordance
with Christian principles will be fuller of joy, peace, love, and so
on? Thus the temptation is to swing away from the non-descriptivist
position of Hare to an analysis of theological statements which
takes them to be not only falsifiable in principle but even conclusively falsifiable in practice. This viewpoint is seldom consistently
maintained, however, for precisely the reasons which Flew himself
describes. By what criterion can we determine whether a life is or
is not lived "genuinely" by Christian principles? If the "fruits of
the spirit" never come to a person, is it just to test the willing soul
that God withholds his blessing? David Cox, as we have already
seen, denies that verification here is ever a "simple matter." Can
we ever be sure that faith was really complete, commitment really
unreserved, if the "experiment" is not a "success"? But surely this
qualification serves to take back with one hand what seems to be
given with the other. Christian love is offered as a cure for all of
man's social ills; if success is not forthcoming from what seem to
be attempts to apply it to man's problems, it is observed that love
was not "really tried." Often those who thunder loudest on behalf
of the factual descriptiveness of theological discourse are the very
ones who withdraw fastest from admitting failure when their
cherished beliefs are put to the test and apparently found wanting.

The fourth position agrees with those who object to the views
of Mitchell and Hare. It insists that theological statements are
assertions and that they can be falsified as conclusively as can any
factual assertion. But (a qualification is added) this falsification is
only possible in principle, not in practice, because the evidence
which alone could settle the issue is *ex hypothesi* available only
after death. Ian Crombie and John Hick are two who have held
this position with considerable effectiveness. Crombie says:

Does anything count against the assertion that God is merciful? Yes,
suffering. Does anything count decisively against it? No, we reply, because
it is true. Could anything count decisively against it? Yes, suffering which
was utterly, eternally and irredeemably pointless. Can we then design
a crucial experiment? No, because we can never see all of the picture.[9]

Hick devotes a good deal of attention to the problem raised—even to those who believe in an afterlife—by Crombie's final phrase: "we can never see all of the picture." Does this phrase entail that never in all eternity will there be a reliable answer to the theistic question? Hick's partial reply is that "although there would probably prove to be a psychological limit to faith, it is important to note that there could be no *logical* limit, no assignable point beyond which faith would become irrational."[10] Still, he adds, "the essence of verification is the exclusion of rational doubt,"[11] and, if the afterlife should be a reality, the intersubjective experience of social existence in the Kingdom of God (combined, perhaps, with an experience of Beatific Vision) would suffice to verify theism. It is possible, then, to conceive what sort of experience would tend to verify (and, conversely, what would falsify) theological assertions. Therefore, Hick believes, the logic of theological discourse is to be factually meaningful even if not falsifiable in practice in this life.

It may be questioned whether Hick's version of the role of verification, which makes of it more a psychological than a logical requirement, is entirely adequate; but despite flaws it would seem that this fourth approach to the logical status of theological discourse with respect to falsification has most to commend it *if* the basic tenet of verificational analysis is correct that all assertions gain their meaningfulness from relevance to actual or possible specific perceptual experiences. Flew's whole presentation of the problem of falsification rests on an assumption that such is the case. But this is to assume the verification principle as an adequate criterion for the meaning of all assertions. And it is precisely this most crucial—and, for verificational analysis, utterly basic—point that we cannot legitimately take for granted.

The verification principle may be of considerable usefulness in many contexts, but it is utterly misunderstood if it is taken as "the" criterion for judging the meaningfulness of all language. An embarrassing example of an assertion which is not meaningful when tested by the verification principle is—the assertion of the verification principle itself! The statement that the meaning of any proposition will be found either in verbal rules (if the proposition is analytic) or in equivalent statements referring to actual or possible sense-experiences (if the proposition is synthetic) seems to be asserting a fact, not offering a definition or a rule of usage. But if the verification principle is not itself analytic, what actual or possible sense-experiences could be relevant to its verification or falsification? No such experience will even in principle be relevant to the task! Indeed, sense-experience alone cannot even recognize the elementary logical distinction between "analytic" and "synthetic" statements *qua* marks on paper or noises uttered by a larynx; much less can it verify assertions about the logical character of their significance. On the basis of the verification principle, therefore, the verification principle is devoid of literal meaning!

Some philosophers have taken the bull by the horns and accepted the verdict—but have insisted that if this is the case then the principle is "useful nonsense." Others have retreated to the position that the verification principle is, after all, really a definition. The latter move, however, means that those who prefer to adopt alternative verbal conventions concerning "meaning" are entirely free to do so, since definitions, for verificational analysis, are not reports of "the way things are." And the former position, by letting the bars down to some "nonsense," opens the gates once more to all the philosophical "chaff" which it had been the function of verificational analysis to eliminate. A wider understanding of meaning, including and interpreting the verification principle, is called for by the needs of this principle itself.

Without a wider theory of meaning, the verification principle is self-stultifying, but if such a theory can be supplied, the verification principle may be retained as a useful instrument for dealing with language which intends to refer to perceptible events or for deciding whether or not statements are *empirically* informative. But in that capacity the verification principle is not a principle which somehow sits in judgment upon all discourse, including theological, ethical, and other non-empirical languages; it is one tool among others and, like all tools, it may not be an appropriate one for all jobs.

What we have here, then, is not really a criterion of meaningfulness (a way of separating wheat from chaff) but a criterion of empiricality (a way, as we might say, of separating wheat from oats, or barley, or rice).[12]

The limited range of the verification principle, on which verificational analysis rests, may explain the failure of this form of linguistic analysis to appreciate the comprehensibility of a wide variety of linguistic uses not amenable to this criterion of meaning. The single-minded devotion of verificational analysis to the verification principle of meaning has resulted in an unfortunately narrow concept of the nature and function of perfectly significant language. In this, verificational analysis has restricted itself by its dogmatic apriorism. Let us examine some of the fruits of the failure to follow the genuinely empirical techniques on which, ironically, verificational analysis most prides itself.

First, major assumptions are adopted before language, in the concrete, is ever approached; and on the basis of these assumptions language is forced into the procrustean bed of pre-established theory. Verificational analysis assumes that the primary function of language is to inform. It assumes that there are only two possible kinds of cognitively meaningful proposition, the analytic and the synthetic. It assumes that all language not meaningful in one or other of these two ways is "merely emotive." Are all these assumptions correct? Open-minded investigation, not the needs of the philosophical system, should determine our answer. The image one gets of verificational analysis is too much that of a sausage grinder, receiving a great variety of cuts of meat but turning out a neat row of uniform *wurst*. Language theory, unlike sausage machines, must not ignore real differences in its raw material for the sake of the working of the machine or the neatness of the end product.

Second, verificational analysis operates on the basis of an un-criticized evaluation of importance. Language is approached with certain paradigms of discourse in mind: most typically these are straightforward, factually informative sentences like "Dinner is ready," or "It is raining." Above all, the paradigm of language is found to be scientific discourse. Thus all other functions of language are implicitly evaluated on the basis of the question "To what extent does this use of language support this 'basic' function of language?" Analytic propositions help language to communicate empirical facts, and so pass the test; others fail to measure up to the imposed yardstick and are rejected, castigated, or treated as negligible.

A more empirical, less doctrinaire approach to language would show that there are many noteworthy functions of language besides the analytic and the empirically informative. Among these are the imperative, performative, and interrogative functions of speech. The function of the imperative, first, is not to inform someone about facts (even facts about his desires—one may be in a military chain of command giving orders quite in conflict with one's own wishes) but to get something done. Imperative uses of language are meaningful—we are able to use them successfully to accomplish our purposes—and yet they are not open to the application of the verification principle of meaning. To the imperative "Open the door," it is logically inappropriate to reply "Prove it!" or "What actual or possible experience would be relevant to verifying that statement?" The performative use of language, secondly, is not uncommon; its function is actually to *do* something. A declaration of war, an official proclamation of the opening of a new highway—such uses of language are themselves acts. Once again we find meaningful language outside the logical scope of the verification principle of meaning. In response to the words "I pronounce you man and wife," or "I hereby name this ship the *Arabella,*" it is not appropriate to ask for verification or falsification. Speech here is not being used to inform but to perform. Yet it is meaningful. The interrogative use of language, third, is not in any way informative. It does not always state that the questioner is ignorant of the answer, since he may be merely testing the person addressed; it does not always state that he wants an answer, because the question may be one which he thinks to be without an answer or to have an answer which he would prefer not to know; a question does not even always function as an imperative—though it often may—since questions may be voiced when one is alone, or musing, or not being listened to. Common speech everywhere exhibits logical structures radically different from verificational analysis's paradigm-language of descriptive factual statements; but common speech is none the less fully capable of accomplishing its various ends and must therefore *in some sense* be judged meaningful.

The gist of this discussion has been to show that there are important realms of discourse with which verificational analysis can deal only awkwardly, if at all. It is now most clearly an open question whether—or to what extent—the critiques which we have seen launched upon theological discourse from the perspective of verificational analysis have resulted in a distortion rather than a clarification of the logic of theological speech.

Certainly we are required to reconsider the argument that theological speech, because of its essential "incomprehensibility," fails even to provide a basis for belief or disbelief. Bernard Williams' claim to this effect (noted in Chapter Three) rests, of course, on evident truth. There is no such thing as a perfectly pellucid discussion of theological matters—nor is there any hope for talk about God which will be as unquestionably clear as talk about tables and chairs. Theological tradition itself recognizes this to be the case and takes steps, variously, to deal with it. But we must not equate, as Williams does, "incomprehensible" with "insignificant." A proposition which is not fully comprehensible need not be *entirely* without significance. The degree of theoretical comprehensibility required for a proposition depends on the function intended for it. Even empirically descriptive statements, about electricity, for example, can retain elements of incomprehensibility and still be useful to physicists and housewives. We can believe or disbelieve such statements even though we do not "properly understand" them in the sense of total and complete theoretical grasp.

The logical use of theological statements is to an important extent theoretical, as we shall see, but this one function need not—as Williams seems to assume—exhaust the uses of theological discourse. And if there are more uses for theological assertions than theoretical belief alone, perhaps even a high degree of theoretical incomprehensibility is compatible with the meaningful employment of such language.[13]

Verificational analysis demands clear and distinct ideas modeled on the precision of logic and the determinateness of sense-experience; but we have come to suspect that this is not a necessary condition for all varieties of meaning. Verificational analysis recognizes as meaningful only the functions of language which are useful for the communication of "fact" in the limited sense of the word which it adopts; but we have suggested that this may be evidence of indefensible narrowness. For a more adequate treatment of theological discourse we must abandon the closely circumscribed techniques of verificational analysis and search for a style of linguistic analysis which can better appreciate the extraordinary variety of the functions of language.

5

THE LOGIC OF
FUNCTIONAL ANALYSIS

THE MORE FLEXIBLE analytical approach to language is represented in modern philosophy by what I shall call "functional analysis." It, like verificational analysis, shares the background of the linguistic philosophy "family." But it conceives in ways very different from those of verificational analysis the nature of language, meaning, and philosophical methods of analysis.

I

A root difference between functional and verificational analysis with far-reaching consequences may be found in the differing models under which each views language. This divergence begins as a matter of emphasis: where verificational analysis tends to conceive of language largely on the model of a useful *invention,* functional analysis tends to picture language more as a natural growth or an *organism.* To say this is not to suppose that functional analysis fails to recognize that some language is a deliberately shaped tool of man or to accuse verificational analysis of never admitting the natural origins of language; but when it comes to describing the essential character of language, the two streams of thought within the linguistic philosophy "family" part company.

While verificational analysis, as we have seen, finds in the statements of the empirical sciences the most adequate examples of what language really is at its best (and draws premature conclusions from this valuation concerning the functioning of "language proper"), Ludwig Wittgenstein in his later writings graphically pictures "language proper" as something quite different from its "surrounding" areas of scientific precision.

Our language can be seen as an ancient city: a maze of little streets and squares, of old and new houses, and of houses with additions from various periods; and this surrounded by a multitude of new boroughs with straight regular streets and uniform houses.[1]

Such a shifting of the models under which language is to be conceived forces quite a different attitude on the investigator. If, with verificational analysis, language is initially pictured as an instrument whose *essential* function is to make possible the communication of empirical facts, then conceptual shears are supplied to snip off those utterances which fail to further this function. But let language be approached, with functional analysis, as a natural phenomenon, and no *a priori* grounds are given for excluding any of the uses of language. Thus functional analysis cannot permit one to approach language in the mood of a technician prepared to select the apparatus which seems most useful for a specific purpose, but advocates, rather, the attitude of a biologist prepared simply to observe and classify. Wittgenstein, the former verificational analyst, wryly reflects on his own earlier and, he thinks, over-orderly conception of "language-games" in the following words:

Review the multiplicity of language-games in the following examples, and in others:

Giving orders, and obeying them—
Describing the appearance of an object, or giving its measurements—
Constructing an object from a description (a drawing)—
Reporting an event—
Speculating about an event—
Forming and testing a hypothesis—
Presenting the results of an experiment in tables and diagrams—
Making up a story; and reading it—
Play-acting—
Singing catches—
Guessing riddles—
Making a joke; telling it—
Solving a problem in practical arithmetic—
Translating from one language into another—
Asking, thanking, cursing, greeting, praying—
—It is interesting to compare the multiplicity of the tools in language and of the ways they are used, the multiplicity of kinds of word and sentence, with what logicians have said about the structure of language. (Including the author of the *Tractatus Logico-Philosophicus*).[2]

Such an empirical view of language would not deny the importance of analytic and synthetic propositions in the daily functioning of language, but it would less grudgingly admit to full linguistic citizenship sentences which verificational analysis would consider alien, or at best naturalized citizens of the linguistic community. Indeed, it might even question the evaluation of importance made by verificational analysis if defended on the basis of frequency of use; perhaps the uses of language which verificational analysts put to one side as "unimportant exceptions" are actually as much to be reckoned with as the empirically factual uses which occupy so much of their attention.

The stress of the functional analyst on language as a "natural growth" leads to a corresponding emphasis on the essential sociality of language, since it is only in and through society that language may be said to have "grown naturally." A private definition of a word does not form part of language because it has none of the results which are the mark of genuine linguistic uses; such a private word would literally make no difference. It would be of as little consequence as would be the right hand's "making a gift" to the left hand!

Why can't my right hand give my left hand money?—My right hand can put it into my left hand. My right hand can write a deed of gift and my left hand a receipt.—But the further practical consequences would not be those of a gift. When the left hand has taken the money from the right, etc., we shall ask: "Well, and what of it?" And the same could be asked if a person had given himself a private definition of a word. . . .[3]

What are the "practical consequences" of essentially social language? Where the ready reply of verificational analysis to this question might have been: "to make possible the growth of factual knowledge, as in the sciences," functional analysis allows itself no single answer at all. What *single* characteristic result have such diverse uses of language as making up a story and reading it, or guessing riddles, or reporting an event, or making a joke and telling it, or greeting, or praying? There is none. The one general characteristic of linguistic utterance is that it has some social context and some practical effects. Sometimes, it is true, we try to employ language where it has no social context or results, but in each case we find that we are violently tearing language out of its ordinary and proper role in the affairs of life; when we examine the task of philosophical analysis we shall see what problems may be caused by such a gratuitous removal of language from its matrix in social existence. *Language, for functional analysis, is a complex social product with many legitimate uses.*

II

The words "uses" and "functions" have for some time now appeared rather frequently in these pages. It is to the cluster of thoughts associated with these words that we must turn when we attempt to uncover the theory of meaning advanced by functional analysis.

Happily deprived of the relatively simple and clear-cut understanding of language possessed by verificational analysis, functional analysis finds that the meaning of "meaning" must be correspondingly more inclusive than that allowed by the principle of verification. In reaction against the excessive concentration of verificational analysis on "meaning" narrowly understood, some philosophers employing the techniques of functional analysis cry, "Don't ask for the meaning, ask for the use." But such a slogan is raised, not, as it would appear, to discard altogether discussion of meaning, but to urge (with, perhaps, the emphasis of overstatement and paradox) the consideration of a new conception of meaning itself. Where verificational analysis wields a rigid yardstick against which to determine the meaning of all assertions, functional analysis provides a flexible tape measure which will, it is claimed, fit not only the plane surfaces of language but also its irregular contours. Functional analysis would approach each sentence as an individual case and with no preconceived definitions of significance. The willingness of verificational analysis to import such a definition, functional analysts feel, betrays the common ground concerning the function of philosophy supposedly shared by all members of the modern philosophical "family."

It is surely no part of philosophy to offer definitions which delimit beforehand the range of meaningfulness. The belief that such is part of the function of philosophy is a relic of the belief which the positivists themselves have done so much to dispel, namely the belief that philosophy, to use the modern idiom, can be more than analysis.[4]

If we were to take quite literally the warning of the functional analysts against all general definitions of meaning, we should be unable to discuss a "theory of meaning" at all! Fortunately, however, a distinction may be made between those more dogmatic "definitions of meaning" which, in the manner of verificational analysis, make explicit *a priori* some standard to be attained by each meaningful sentence and other, more empirical, general statements of procedure which instruct us where to look in each case to discover the meaning of the sentence. The "theory of meaning" of functional analysis may therefore be understood as fundamentally a statement of procedure: *the meaning of language,* we are told, *is found in its use.*

"Look at the sentence as an instrument, and at its sense as its employment."[5] "Every sign *by itself* seems dead. *What* gives it life? —In use it is *alive*. Is life breathed into it there?—Or is the *use* its life?"[6] "The arrow points only in the application that a living being makes of it."[7]

If the meaning of a statement is to be found in its use, how are we to understand "use"? One possible interpretation of "use" would emphasize its link with "usage," wherein popular usage may be tabulated roughly, it would seem, on the basis of the educated consensus. An influential example of conceptual analysis based on considerations of current correct usage of language is Professor J. L. Austin's article "Other Minds,"[8] in which the concept of knowledge is approached through an examination of the proper usage of the verb "to know." But, protesting against a possible overemphasis on "usage," Professor Gilbert Ryle reminds us that it is philosophically risky merely to point to the fact that "nobody says ——." Use, according to Ryle, should be interpreted as more closely akin to "standard correct employment" than to "popular usage."

There cannot be a misusage any more than there can be a miscustom or a misvogue. The methods of discovering linguistic usages are the methods of philologists.[9]

These two interpretations, however, need not be mutually exclusive. We must not say

. . . *either* that philosophy is only a conceptual investigation *or* that philosophers should investigate only the ordinary concepts of common sense *or* that they should never try to improve any of the concepts they have investigated (which would necessarily involve changing the present use of the words concerned).[10]

"Yet," the last-quoted writer adds, "it is surely only prudent to elucidate the current nature of the concept (the current correct usage of the word and its synonyms—and any equivalents in any other language) before rushing forward with suggestions on how to reform it."[11]

Whatever their internal differences of interpretation, functional analysts close ranks in rejection of the doctrinaire standard of meaning embodied in the verification principle—if this principle is inflated into the measure of all language. The attempt at verification, as we have recognized, may under many circumstances be useful as an aid to classification. But:

> To say of a given sentence that it can be verified is not to say anything about the meaningfulness of the sentence but to characterize it as being a sentence of a certain type, namely, an empirical sentence.[12]

If the verification principle cannot deal with a sentence, this cannot be construed as sufficient justification for concluding that the sentence is either analytic or lacking in all significance. Admittedly,

> . . . such a sentence cannot be an empirical one. The question whether it is meaningful is a further question, quite independent of the question whether it is empirical or not.[13]

Meaning, then, is more adequately understood in terms of the uses or functions of language than in terms of actual or possible experiences. It may often be the function of language to refer to some experience or perceptible event, but it need not always be so. The more inclusive approach to meaning is clearly exhibited in the philosophical practice of functional analysis.

III

The task of functional analysis is both to elucidate the meaning of language by revealing its use or uses in context and to uncover linguistic misuses when they occur. Wittgenstein places much emphasis on the latter role of philosophical analysis. "Philosophical problems arise," he says, "when language *goes on holiday*."[14] "The confusions which occupy us arise when language is like an engine idling, not when it is doing work."[15] Language has a tendency sometimes to slip from doing useful work into idle habitual repetitions which have no use. How many puzzling questions and answers are based on verbal wheel-spinning where the language involved is divorced from the context in which it had a real function! St. Augustine's famous concern about the paradoxes of time[16] strikes many functional analysts as an example of this misuse of language since the philosophical puzzlement in which he is caught is due to his attempted use of temporal language far afield from the contexts where it has some use: for example, of being early to dinner or late for a dental appointment or on time for a dress parade. The role of philosophical analysis is upon each occurrence of this misuse to point out the distance between the confused employment of language which is causing the "mental cramp" and the concrete setting-in-function from which the puzzling language was torn.

But necessary as this role for functional analysis must be when needless puzzles are generated by the misuse of language, the occasions on which language goes entirely "on holiday" are relatively infrequent. More important work is done by functional analysis when it clarifies the actual uses of language of various sorts. Two related techniques are often used to aid in this important task: the paradigm case technique and the technique of significant comparison.

The usefulness of the paradigm case technique in clarifying the function of puzzling or problem-causing discourse is in its simplicity, directness, and universal availability. Whenever one is confronted with a word, phrase, or sentence whose function is unclear or controversial, one may deal with it by the paradigm case technique by bringing forward another example of the same word or sentence which is perfectly clear as to use. This uncontroversial example will be taken as the paradigm-use of the language in question, and study of the paradigm in relation to the puzzling example will greatly clarify the latter's logical role. One thing is clear: there will somewhere be a paradigm for any phrase, because without *some* genuine and legitimate use that phrase could not exist.

This fact is not always recognized. Occasionally, for example, someone who is deeply impressed with modern physics may wonder whether any legitimate use of the word "solid" can remain. Every physical object, he may muse to himself, is a whirling mass of electrical charges; nothing is really solid; my desk, this stone wall —these are not "really" *solid*. But in raising these questions the person is leading himself into confusion. The very paradigm-uses of the word "solid" are those with reference to stone walls and desks. Uses in these contexts are the very uses that *are the meaning* of the expression. To suggest that these meaning-bestowing uses are themselves inappropriate is absurd and, in a sense, contradictory. What may be learned from this application of the paradigm case technique is that the meaning of "solid" is in no way incompatible with "composed wholly of whirling electrical charges." Denying this is equivalent to denying that any use whatever pertains to "solid"—that is, concluding that it is a meaningless expression. But the fact that we can *use* "solid" correctly, distinguishing solid things from liquid or gaseous or squashy things, refutes this claim.

In addition to the paradigm case technique, functional analysis employs a technique which I have called "significant comparison," a tool of considerable usefulness in revealing the meaning of our language. If a phrase is unclear, it is often wise policy to compare the job it accomplishes with other forms of language—or other activities—that do the same work. Such a technique often throws much light on the meaning of a statement. It may considerably clarify the meaning of the statement (made by the Mayor) "I hereby declare this expressway open" if we utilize the technique of significant comparison to show that this sentence has the same function as, for example, the Mayor's ceremonial cutting of a ribbon or swinging open of a gate. What was the use of the Mayor's statement? Was it to inform us about an event which had occurred five minutes, one minute, a split second before he spoke? No, the expressway was not officially open until the Mayor *had* spoken. Was his statement a disguised plea for us to use the new highway? Hardly! The logical use of this language was to bring about the official opening of the road; its meaning is misunderstood in other terms. And one of the best helps in grasping this meaning is to compare the Mayor's speech with other means of accomplishing the same end.

Above all, functional analysis insists that those who use the language under study should be allowed to express their own views as to the function of their speech. Before the poet, for example, is told *ex cathedra* what uses his language has, he should be asked how he *intends* to employ his words. The empiricism on which functional analysis rightly prides itself will be preserved only if a fair hearing is given to those who are most intimately involved in the use of language under analysis.

For an understanding of theological discourse, therefore, the principles of functional analysis require that we listen to the explanation offered by theologians themselves concerning their language. While listening we must keep our critical wits about us, of course, because the ability to use a form of speech does not guarantee an adequate understanding of the logical principles underlying this use; but we cannot afford to be without the insights concerning theological discourse which those most concerned with its use can offer. The next three chapters, therefore, will deal with three theological viewpoints concerning the language of theism. When we have acquainted ourselves with these positions we shall be better prepared to take up again the thread of functionally analytical philosophical discussion and to see why it is that some functional analysts condemn theological language as serving an "improper" function, others claim to identify certain familiar functions in this language, and still others insist that theological speech has a function uniquely its own.

6

THE LOGIC OF ANALOGY

THE FUNDAMENTAL PROBLEM for users of theological language, as seen by one theological tradition,* is the avoidance, on the one hand, of anthropomorphism and, on the other, of agnosticism. Let us examine the problem as it is visualized by these theologians.

I

Human language, all admit, is best suited for dealing with familiar objects, qualities, and relations. The very meanings of the terms in our speech—as illustrated by the paradigm case technique —have grown up through the needs and experiences of ordinary life. Since our language is thus firmly rooted in human purpose, it would seem inevitable that wherever it is applied it must express its ancestry by imposing human categories of thought on everything it touches. But if human speech brings with its use unavoidable anthropocentric distortion, how is anthropomorphism to be avoided in theological discourse?

God is traditionally held to be "infinite," of course, and lip service is paid to his "transcendent and unimaginable glory"; but despite these verbal bows in the direction of God's "otherness," language developed to deal with finite objects is used to describe him—and at times to do so in considerable detail! The inexorable pressures of language would seem to prevent anyone from speaking about the infinite or the transcendent but, rather, to force one to

---

* Logical traditions, not ecclesiastical or confessional traditions, are here under discussion. I am also particularly concerned with contemporary interpreters of this tradition rather than with historical questions of origin or exegesis, which would take us too far afield.

speak—despite oneself—less of infinite God than of superlative man.

Let one speak of God as "the All-Wise One," for example, and his language compels him to understand the "wisdom" of God in the same sense that human wisdom is understood (though greatly magnified, no doubt) *if he is to understand anything at all* by these words; this is the only sense of the word that human beings can know. Even the traditional recourse to the "theistic proofs," if looked to as providing words which are straightforwardly applicable to God, must fail, since (even if the proofs were valid) to prove God a "first cause" or an "unmoved mover" or "sum of perfections" or "self-existing being" is either to deal in human language and in human meanings, or not. On the first alternative "God" becomes merely a part of the natural order, "for clearly causes and effects are terms in a single series and belong to the same order of reality,"[1] and God's perfections are reduced to the level delimited by human imagination. On the second alternative "cause," "mover," "perfection," "existing," "being," and the like, are emptied of meaning when predicated of God.

> You are in fact in an insoluble dilemma. If you assert existence and causality of God in the same sense in which you assert them of finite beings, you are rendering God incapable of fulfilling the very function for whose performance you alleged him to be necessary. But if you assert existence and causality of God in an altogether different sense from that in which you assert them of finite beings, you are making statements about God to which you can, *ex hypothesi,* assign no intelligible content. God therefore is either useless or unthinkable; this would seem to be the conclusion of the matter.[2]

The theist is caught in a cross fire. Either human language is allowed to retain its meaning, drawn from human experience of the finite, in which case it cannot be about the God of theism, who is not supposed either to be finite or to be properly describable in finite terms; or language, "purified" of its anthropocentric roots, is emptied of meaning for human beings, in which case it can be neither human language nor—for us—"about" God. Put more technically, the theist would seem compelled to choose between *univocal* language, which makes the object of his talk no longer "God" because merely comparable to the rest of his experience, and *equivocal* language, which "cleanses" the terms used in describing God entirely of any anthropomorphism they might ordinarily possess but thereby forces the theist into a position of total agnosticism, capable of knowing nothing as to the *meaning* of his words-about-God—not even knowing whether "existence" when applied to "God" has any relationship to its ordinary human use. From the standpoint of logic, the theist who chooses to speak in equivocal terms is only punning on the English language when he calls God "good" or "loving" or "wise." Apart from sheerly emotional factors, he should have no objection, on this position, to speaking of God as "pink" (in a "completely different sense") or "multicellular" or "washable" (in senses "wholly uncontaminated with their ordinary meanings").

There seems no escape. If univocal, then language falls into anthropomorphism and cannot be about *God;* if equivocal, then language bereft of its meaning leads to agnosticism and cannot for us be *about* God. But at this point it is the contention of a major theological tradition that between the univocal and the equivocal lies a third logically important employment of language which can provide theological discourse with a live alternative to both anthropomorphism and agnosticism. This "middle way" is the logic of analogy.

II

"Analogy is a relation between objects," says Austin Farrer, "capable of being classed as a species of 'likeness.' " The sort of "likeness" on which any analogy depends, he continues, is that which is "reducible to the presence in the similars of an identical abstractible characteristic."[3] If this is the case, then subscribing to the logic of analogy concerning statements about God would entail our accepting the proposition that there is at least one abstractible characteristic which God, in some legitimate sense, can be said to share with finite being. The function of a theory of analogy on this interpretation must be to explain in *what* "legitimate sense" or senses such a characteristic would be predicated of God. We shall have occasion later to question the objectivist view of analogy which is offered here, but since the traditional account given of this logic has been in terms of a "theological object-language" it will be useful to follow the exposition of this viewpoint in traditional terms.

Two kinds of analogies are distinguished as relevant to theism. The first, usually called the "analogy of attribution," relates two analogates which may in many respects differ widely from each other. One of the analogates (the prime analogate) possesses the characteristic predicated of it in a "formal" manner, that is, in a wholly proper (univocal) and actual sense, while the other analogate has predicated of it a "like" characteristic in a relative or derivative sense. Some example like the following is often chosen to illustrate this variety of analogy: we may call both men and mountain resorts "healthy." The place may be called "healthy" in a derivative sense thanks to its tendency to cause the men who live there (the prime analogates in this case) to be called "healthy" in a formal sense. This is a good example since it shows not only what is meant by "formal" and "derivative" predication in the terminology of the classical doctrine of analogy but also the importance for the very possibility of the analogy of the *real relation* in which the analogates stand. No analogy of attribution can be manufactured out of thin air; there must be some prior relationship between the terms on the basis of which common attribution is possible. Nor does the theological use of the analogy of attribution admit exception to this rule. "In its theological application, where the analogates concerned are God and a creature, the relation upon which the analogy is based will be that of creative causality; creatures are related to God as his effects. . . ."[4] Once it is made clear that the theist bases his language about God on the understanding that God is creative cause of finite things (it is held) there should be no obstacle to admitting that theological language founded on this real relation is fully meaningful by virtue of the analogy of attribution.

In addition to the analogy of attribution there may be distinguished another theologically useful kind of analogy traditionally called the "analogy of proportionality." While the analogates composing an analogy of attribution are "unequal," that is, only one of the two really deserving to have predicated of it the common abstractible characteristic (the "analogue") in a *formal* sense, both the terms in an analogy of proportionality possess the analogue in a literal and unmetaphorical sense. But each possesses it only *proportionately to the nature* of the analogates concerned.

If, on the one hand, one were to speak of himself as "feeling blue" or of the air as "blue" with invective, he would (strictly speaking) be equivocating. The analogy of proportionality would stand closer to univocal speech than this. If, on the other hand, one were to call identically colored wallpaper in different rooms "blue," language here would be used univocally. Analogy must insert itself between the two. By means of an analogy of proportionality, to continue the illustration, I might call the sky "blue" and my wife's eyes "blue"; here both terms possess the common characteristic *formally, but in the way appropriate to their distinctive natures*. My wife's eyes are blue with a "blueness" literally appropriate to human eyes and not to the sky; the sky is blue with a "blueness" literally appropriate to an August day and not to a human eye. In this way analogy, we are told, is able to strike a middle way between univocal and equivocal language. "In the strict sense, an analogy of proportionality implies that the analogue under discussion is found formally in each of the analogates but in a mode that is determined by the nature of the analogate itself."[5]

The application of analogy of proportionality to theological discourse is straightforward: a term predicated of God belongs properly to *his* nature, in a way proportionate to his nature, in the same way that a term predicated of one of his creatures belongs properly to *its* nature, in a way proportionate to its nature. Man is "good" in a way literally appropriate to man's finite nature. Thus, the classical doctrine concludes, "God's goodness" is neither something unrelated to "man's goodness" nor merely identical to human virtue. A similar analogy of proportionality would be found to hold between each of the qualities and attributes which could be predicated of divinity. In this sense,

. . . while there cannot be a proportion of the finite to the infinite, there can be within both the finite and the infinite proportions which are similar. Thus the divine goodness is to God as human goodness is to man, and the divine wisdom is to God as human wisdom is to man, and, in general, the divine attributes are to God as the analogous finite qualities are to finite things.[6]

III

This means of avoiding the dilemma confronting theological discourse through a "middle way" can, with proper interpretation, be of value to modern students of theological language; but a

recognition of the many shortcomings of the approach must pre-
cede any genuine appreciation of the logic of analogy.

First, the analogy of proportionality suffers from serious difficulties. Superficially it seems that true proportionality is affirmed
for the analogates, but, as E. L. Mascall points out, at no point
may an unambiguous "equals" sign be placed between the terms
of the pseudo proportion. Mascall illustrates this difficulty in terms
of an analogy of proportionality between the "life" of cabbages
and the "life" of men (here assuming "life" not to be a univocal
term). At first, he says, a univocal sense is denied to the meaning
of "life" when predicated of men and cabbages in favor of what
appears to be a straightforward proportion: the "life" of a cabbage
is to the nature of the cabbage as the "life" of a man is to his
human nature. But, again, this seeming proportion must be denied
in its simple form because the nature of the cabbage will determine
not only what "life" will be for a cabbage but also *how it will
determine* how it determines what "life" means in a cabbage. And
once the process of determinations is begun there is no stopping it!
The nature of the cabbage (or the man) must forever be allowed
to determine how it will determine how it will determine . . .
whatever it is determining, each stage further removed from any
approach to univocal meaning, each stage finding the analogates
separated by greater and greater distances from each other. At this
point the bewildered thinker despairs! "For the fact remains that
we have denied that our equal signs really stand for equality and
we have not indicated anything definite that they do stand for."[7]

A still more serious objection to the theological application of
the analogy of proportionality is that the peculiarities of the theistic
problems make this form of analogy able to "deliver" far less than
it would seem to promise. We are offered what looks like a simple
calculation to be worked out (although we have seen that it cannot
be expected to be worked out as a mathematical problem might
be): but if we try actually to employ the steps which it seems to
recommend in order to learn the literal meaning of words predicated of God, we discover that the "proportion" is irreducible
since there are *two,* not one, "unknowns." "The quality x_1 is to
man's nature in man in the same respect that this quality x_2 is to
God's nature in God," we are informed. But though we have a fair
idea as to what is meant by "man's nature" and what might be

literally "appropriate" or "proportional" to it, we stumble in the dark when we try to conceive "God's nature" in the same way in order to have an idea of what could be "literally appropriate" to *it*. In place of "God's nature"—infinitely different, we are told, from all his finite effects—we might equally well substitute another letter symbolizing a second "unknown" in what already has proved a pseudo equation: "x_1 is to man's nature in much the same way as x_2 is to y." What has happened to our "middle way" of analogy? The "proportion" which was to throw light on the meaning of our terms has been exposed as unworkable; worse, if taken seriously it would appear to license the wildest equivocation on the basis of the infinite gap which yawns between the analogates. The only way this consequence could be avoided, it appears, would be to discover some literal truth about the "nature of God," as many have hoped to do through the "theistic proofs," whereby the pseudo proposition could be "worked." But this literal sort of knowledge, as we have seen, is unattainable.

Analogies of attribution, we may be told, sometimes span great diversity between analogates: but even this capacity is unable to establish theological discourse on firm logical ground. Analogies of attribution, unlike those of proportionality, are unconcerned with the formal or proper character of more than one of their analogates. They are content merely to state that the analogue is predicated of the secondary analogate in a "derived" sense based on a real relation. If the relation between the analogates is that of cause and effect, for example, then the analogy of attribution allows us to apply the name of the characteristic possessed formally in the prime analogate to the secondary analogate solely because of the latter's power to *cause* the predicated characteristic. A mountain resort is called "healthy" not because it possesses that particular predicate formally but simply because of its ability to *produce* health (literally understood) in men. Thus, in scholastic terminology, the mountain resort is "virtually" rather than formally healthy.

But this means that the analogy of attribution allows us to remain in ignorance of the formal nature of one of the analogates; our aim, on the contrary, was to speak of these very formal characteristics of God and somehow to justify our language about them. The analogy of attribution tells us nothing we did not know before: it merely tells us that whatever is capable of producing an effect may

have applied to it ("virtually") the term properly signifying that
effect thanks solely to the fact that—it is able to produce that
effect. In other words, whatever can produce an effect can produce
an effect! Such an analogy can tell us nothing concerning God
which theists had not accepted beforehand—that he is the *cause* of
finite phenomena.

Thus when we say that God and Mr. Jones are both good or that they
are both beings, remembering that the content which the word "good"
or "being" has for us is derived from our experience of the goodness and
the being of creatures, we are, so far as analogy of attribution is concerned, saying no more than that God has goodness or being in whatever
way is necessary if he is to be able to produce goodness and being in his
creatures. This would not seem necessarily to indicate anything more
than that the perfections which are found formally in various finite modes
in creatures exist *virtually* in God, that is to say, that he is able to produce them in the creatures; it does not seem to necessitate that God
possesses them formally himself.[8]

The analogy of attribution seems entirely redundant if its true
purpose is to inform us as to the meaning of words referring to real
properties possessed by God, since, as Dorothy Emmet points out,
"the appropriateness of the analogy depends on the reality of the
relation which it exemplifies. The existence of the relation cannot
be established by analogical argument; but if there are independent
grounds for asserting it, it can be described analogically."[9]

Analogies of attribution are not only redundant, however; they
are also, even more damagingly, excessively permissive. Far *too
many* predicates may be applied to God. If to be the cause of
something is "virtually" to be characterizable by that predicate,
then, if God is the cause of all things, theists should be willing to
apply *all conceivable predicates* to him in this "virtual" sense. As
the cause of the physical universe he must be (virtually) hot, heavy,
multi-colored, and so on. The analogy of attribution admits of no
control. If some, but not all, of the predicates claimed by this type
of analogy are held to be formally as well as virtually applicable
to God, then what is to distinguish them? Can the theist be content
to admit a method of talking which would seem to make God
"sweet tasting" as well as "good," "finely powdered" as well as
"wise"?

To answer this objection a theist might insist that some of God's "perfections" are formally appropriate to his nature while others are only virtually appropriate. He might try to deduce from "God's nature" which perfections would fall into which class.[10] But to make such deductions, some prior understanding of the words describing "God's nature" is demanded. Once again we find ourselves within a circle from which there appears to be no ready exit.

Does the logic of analogy provide us with a genuine "middle way"? Its original purpose was to mediate between univocality and equivocality, but the results of our inquiry thus far make us wonder whether Aristotle was not correct in classifying analogy as a form of equivocation. More accurately, perhaps, the logic of analogy as we have seen it is a combination of—or a running back and forth between—the two unacceptable extremes. F. C. Copleston acknowledges this point.

It would appear . . . that the theistic philosopher is faced with a dilemma. If he pursues exclusively the negative way, he ends in sheer agnosticism, for he whittles away the positive meaning which a term originally had for him until nothing is left. If, however, he pursues exclusively the affirmative way, he lands in anthropomorphism. But if he attempts to combine the two ways, as indeed he must if he is to avoid both extremes, his mind appears to oscillate between anthropomorphism and agnosticism.[11]

If such oscillation is the inescapable fate of theological language, suspicion is thrown on the logical status of analogy as an independent logical alternative. Can it be that the theist is merely confused and undecided as to which horn of the dilemma he would prefer to be impaled upon?

Not only the conceptual fruits but also the ontological presuppositions of the logic of analogy on its traditional interpretation are vulnerable to criticism. Analogy, on the view expressed earlier by Farrer, depends on there being an identical abstractible characteristic "present in" two beings; but wholly aside from the difficulties inherent in the "theory of universals" which seems to be implicit here, the assumption that God possesses abstractible characteristics identical to some also possessed by men is radically questionable. On the theological level, this assumption has been vigorously rebutted by neo-orthodox and reformed traditions which stress the complete alienation of sinful man from holy God through man's corruption. The depravity of man's very being, on this view, rules

out any possibility of the "analogy of being" which must undergird
the logic of analogy. And, on the philosophical level, the supposition that any identity of characteristic can hold between God and
man is incompatible with the fundamental theistic assumption that
God is infinite. It would appear impossible in principle that any
finite characteristic could be identical with an infinite characteristic.
If there is to be the relation of identity of abstractible characteristic
between man and God, either man's finitude or God's infinitude is
sure to be violated. To maintain these essentials of the theistic view
the ontological foundations on which the logic of analogy rest must
be abandoned.

It is no longer possible, I believe, to hold that the logic of
analogy, as it has normally been interpreted, is cogent. Is there then
no value in this traditional approach to theological discourse? To
determine the answer to this question we must decide whether or
not to allow any interpretation but the traditional, metaphysically
oriented view of analogy to be heard. If we insist on the use of the
"material mode" of speech, requiring analogy to provide us with
information about real properties of supernatural entities, little can
be salvaged. But if we allow ourselves to examine the logic of
analogy as *one means of providing criteria for the disciplined use
of ordinary language in theological contexts,* looking for its value
on the "formal" rather than the "material" mode of speech, much
that may be of interest to us remains.

Put in the "formal" mode, then, the essential problem posed for
the logic of analogy is how human language, despite its anthropocentric nature, may be *given a use* within a theological context
while escaping both the univocality which gives rise to anthropomorphism and the sheer undisciplined meaninglessness of equivocality. Analogy meets this problem by explicating *rules* limiting the
use of words drawn from ordinary non-theological contexts in
formulae containing the word "God" (where "God" entails such
words as "infinite" and "transcendent"). The presence of these
rules makes clear to the user that ordinary speech, if taken without
qualification into the language of theology, will violate the latter
entailments; at the same time, the rules license the use of certain
words, properly at home elsewhere, in theological contexts.

Seen thus, the analogy of attribution states the rule: a word
from a secular context may be used theologically *where there is*

already a ground in the theological "universe of discourse" (authoritative doctrine, dogma, creed, or proposition entailed by one of these) for holding that this quality is derived from God's uniquely characteristic activity. But this rule also warns that the quality designated by the word in question is not to be assumed "formally" applicable to God but only "virtually," as a reminder that within the theological conceptual schema God is taken to be its ultimate source.

The analogy of proportionality, in the formal mode, offers the rule: a word may be borrowed from ordinary speech for use in theological discourse only if it is constantly borne in mind that the word can apply to "God" exclusively in the manner (unimaginable to us) permitted by the fundamental axioms and entailment-rules governing the entire system of theistic talk about "God."

So interpreted, the logic of analogy rests upon no ontological assumption of identity between God and man. It is not vulnerable to criticism from theologians who denounce the *analogia entis* as blasphemy or from philosophers who must insist on the qualitative distinctness of finite and infinite. It is not wounded by reproof for its failure to be informative, because its function is not to inform but, rather, to limit the proper employment of language within the framework of theistic systematic assumptions. To interpret the logic of analogy in this way is to depart from tradition and to abandon much of what metaphysically minded theologians have sought in these doctrines, but the metaphysical value of analogy has in any case been shown to be wanting, while its usefulness for the understanding of the syntactic dimension of theological language* may prove to be considerable.

* See Chap. 12.

7
THE LOGIC OF OBEDIENCE

A SECOND major theological tradition is concerned less about anthropomorphism than about pride and afraid less of agnosticism than of faithlessness. Only in the obedience of faith, this tradition insists, can man's language convey meaning and truth about God. This approach to justifying language in its theological application we shall call, therefore, the logic of obedience; it is held to be a higher rationality than any known to philosophy.

I

Philosophical reason, according to the logic of obedience, is often an occasion for rebellious pride, and as such it must carefully be kept within its proper bounds by the higher logic of theology. Professor T. F. Torrance has put the case for the logic of obedience over against "autonomous natural reason" (maintaining that "it is only by means of faith that philosophy can be kept true to itself"[1]) by restating on theological lines the nature of "objectivity," "criticism," and "rationality."

One of the most common errors of thought abstracted from obedience is the supposition that purely impartial or "objective" thinking is a human possibility. But modern investigation, Torrance says, has abundantly shown that

. . . even the conclusions of our abstract thinking do not really arise from the logical basis on which they seem to repose. They come from something much deeper, a certain habit or set of mind which gives these arguments their real force.[2]

It is at the deepest level that philosophical positions are really formed; they do not issue from the philosopher's conscious mind alone. The insidious fact about the real roots of philosophical thought is that they may not be at all apparent to the thinker himself, who may consider himself the model of objectivity—but is therefore victimized the more by his own uncriticized assumptions. What are these assumptions? Apart from faith, Torrance contends, they are always assumptions antithetical to the Christian view of the world and man; but this, after all, is only to be expected on the basis of the biblical revelation of man's radically evil condition. And these assumptions wreck the very possibility of a theological appeal to "objective analysis," since there is no such thing as "objectivity" in natural human reason; there is only fierce hostility, based on extra-logical factors, toward the Christian revelation. Genuine objectivity, as we shall soon see, is made possible only by obedience.

Modern philosophy has rejected the pretensions of "system-building," Torrance points out, in favor of what is called criticism or analysis. This is a healthful development, but truly critical analytical philosophy is an ideal which is impossible for the human mind to attain unaided. How can a philosophy which is unable to criticize its own determining assumptions, as already noted, succeed in being really critical of anything else? The basis of its critiques has been left uncriticized! "The difficulty is that even the critical philosophers of to-day are almost never conscious of their basic attitude. They adopt it as a fundamental canon of thought."[3] In this way the natural mind's lack of objectivity crushes philosophical hope for genuine criticism. Genuine critical philosophy, in Torrance's view, is also made possible only by obedience.

It is often assumed that reason's internal principles—the law of contradiction, the law of identity, and so on—must be given an entirely "free hand" if the mind is to achieve true rationality. On this view it is imagined that the mind must be governed by no principles or influences outside its own methods and criteria. Such a belief in "autonomous reason" assumes that any and all varieties of subject matter can be comprehended, or at least adequately dealt with, by reason's own categories. Thus

. . . it has become an axiom for the reason to accept as rational only that which fits in with the forms of its own autonomous activity. It refuses to recognize anything outside the charmed circle of its own self-sufficiency except what can be understood by the norms immanent to reason.[4]

This view of reason, however, is rightly suspect in many philosophical quarters. Today reason is increasingly understood to be "not something substantival but verbal, not so much a state as an act, and therefore to be functionally interpreted."[5] And what is the "function" which provides the key to a more accurate understanding of reason? Torrance replies: "Reason is our capacity for objectivity."[6]

The discussion has thus circled back to the nature of "objectivity." What, we may now ask, is this "genuine objectivity"—that for which "reason" is our capacity—which the logic of obedience holds to be beyond the normal powers of the mind?

Torrance at once distinguishes two notions of "objectivity": first, the "ordinary" objectivity of human rationality, operating, by means of logical principles inherent in it, on ordinary subject matter; and, second, "true" objectivity, of which ordinary objectivity is a special case. "True" objectivity is, in Torrance's more fundamental sense, *the capacity for the mind to be conformed to or behave appropriately before its object.*

Relative to most objects confronting us, this criterion of objectivity is sufficiently met in terms of the canons inherent in reason, but the assumption that what is sufficient for *most* is sufficient for *all* possible objects is totally unfounded. Sometimes—Torrance invites us to consider the possibility—the object confronting us may be beyond the powers of our ordinary categories of objectivity; but even then, for the mind to behave truly *objectively* is for it to *act appropriately* before the object. And the appropriate act in such a case is to refuse to apply the inapplicable standards of "ordinary" objectivity. In this refusal, and in it alone, we are behaving in conformity with the character of the object confronting us; only then are we truly objective. If rationality is our capacity for behaving objectively, then in this case we are truly rational only in rejecting the ordinary principles of rationality.

Clearly, Torrance concludes, the confrontation with the Word of God—God's own self acting in revelation to save man—must be the supreme instance of the incompatibility of "ordinary" objectivity (natural reason) with true objectivity (genuine rationality).

When God makes himself known to man, man's mind tries at first to force its new Object into the patterns of "ordinary" objectivity.

But reason is unable to subdue this Divine Subject-Object to ordinary objectivity (*i.e.* to its own subjectivity) for that would not be behaving in terms of the Object. . . . Therefore reason, in order to be truly rational, must suspend its ordinary urge to objectivity, and find its true objectivity in the Divine Person who cannot be subdued to a mere object or resolved into the conclusion of a philosophical argument. This is the trouble with our reason that it is habituated to subduing objects to its own subjectivity.[7]

How, then, shall we describe the "appropriate act" which constitutes true objectivity before the Word of God? It has abandoned the ordinary criteria of objectivity and rationality; what has it left? "Only in the act of acknowledgement," Torrance answers, "can it receive the capacity to behave in terms of the Object, *but must therefore be prepared for transformation in obedience to its unique Subject-Object.*"[8] Rationality in theological matters does not oppose, therefore, but presupposes obedience, since any other response is inappropriate to the Object and *ipso facto* irrational.

If philosophy cannot succeed in objective thinking about fundamental matters apart from a response of obedience to the Word of God, then neither can it hope to be truly *critical* apart from faith. The logic of obedience in faith is presupposed for genuine rationality, objectivity, and criticism, we are told, because faithless would-be philosophers are so bound up in their unconscious assumptions that the objective rationality required for true criticism is beyond their reach.

They cannot think otherwise until there is a fundamental change in their mental make-up, *i.e.* until in faith they are able to stand outside of themselves on the ground of a Word which reaches them from without and not from within.[9]

II

What is the nature of this "Word" which, according to the logic of obedience, makes true rationality possible by "reaching" one from "without" oneself? To understand the justification which this logic offers for human words about God we shall have to examine what is said concerning the divine Word of God as related to physical events, to the Bible, and to the Church.

To comprehend the relation existing, according to the logic of obedience, between Word of God and physical events, we must divest ourselves of the misunderstanding which leads us to suppose that God's revelatory Word is necessarily *verbal*. As a matter of fact, the logic of obedience maintains, the Word of God is in no circumstances a matter of *words only*. The most striking statement of the non-verbal character of God's Word is the affirmation *Jesus Christ is the Word of God*. A man, an event, a concrete life in history is the supreme embodiment of the Word of God, not a proposition or a "truth." Torrance inquires what John Calvin, a fountainhead of the logic of obedience, meant by "Word" and finds, "By Word he meant the Eternal Word who resides in the bosom of the Father, but who has also in the flesh of Jesus Christ become physical event."[10] These two aspects must be held together: the *divine and eternal* nature of the revealing act must be emphasized, for the Word must be from beyond the relativities of history, from the very "bosom of the Father," if it is to be a genuine object of obedience for that faith which transforms one's personality "from without" and makes possible true "objectivity," "criticism," and "rationality"; and, equally, the *concrete and historical* nature of the revealing act must also be retained, because the Word must be a word to men in nature and history and thus must necessarily be received as "flesh" and "physical event." The primary Word of revelation, therefore, is none other than Jesus Christ, eternal Word "become physical event" in our temporal order. How the two poles (divine-human, temporal-eternal) of the Word of God are to be united is the mystery of Incarnation and remains mystery, a mystery before which our most rational response is to abandon the normal criteria of reason in obedience to a wider objectivity than unaided philosophy can attain.

The Bible, for the logic of obedience, is also in some way the Word of God, but that it is so in a derivative sense is made clear by two considerations: first, the Bible is Word of God only in so far as it reveals Christ, the primary Word; and second, Scripture becomes Word of God only upon those occasions when, by inexplicable miracle, God relates his eternal Word to the humble words of the scriptural page through the "Analogy of Christ," that is, in a manner analogous to the mystery of the Incarnation of God in Christ. This second consideration rules out two methods of approaching the words of the Bible which, for obedience, are logically inappropriate. The first, literalism, identifies the actual words of the Bible with God's divine Word, thereby assuming that God's Word can be a possession of men to be boasted of, ignored, misused. By lifting the words of the Bible too high, literalism only succeeds in dragging the Word of God too low. Liberalism, on the other hand, imposes human pretensions to "objectivity" and "rational criticism" upon the words of Scripture, thereby desecrating the holiness of the Holy Scripture. In contrast to liberalism, literalism can be seen by the logic of obedience to have been right "in its insistence that the Word of God is present in the Bible . . . though it was in error in conceiving its presence in a static and material way."[11] Where literalism errs is in failing to recognize the "incarnational" nature of the Word of God in the Bible. Just as Jesus, the primary Word of revelation, was physical event demanding that we "take seriously the fact that the Word has assumed our fallen humanity, and was made in the likeness of sinful flesh,"[12] so the Word revealed in Scripture must be admitted to make use of "fallen" and imperfect means. "The Bible is the Word of God, but it is the Word of God only by the inspiration of God, not by virtue of any property inherent in itself. In itself the Bible consists of human words, which like all such are subject to error."[13] But, on the other hand, just as the Incarnation was God's perfect Word for men, so Scripture *when inspired* becomes transformed from mere words into the Word which demands our obedience.

It is only in the Church, however, that the full interrelationship between divine Word as personal event, as written marks, and as spoken sounds is fully visible. No life of obedience to the Word of God given "once and for all" in Jesus Christ and made known through the Bible can be lived in solitude. An integral part of the Word itself is a call for fellowship, and apart from the community the Word cannot even be known. It is the language of the Church, therefore—in relation to action—which requires our attention.

To say that systematic theology is impossible apart from the life of the faithful community is merely to utter a tautology, because theology, for the logic of obedience, is properly *defined* as a task of the Church: "the task of criticising and revising her language

about God."[14] The Church at times falls into uncertainty as to
what its language should be; it sometimes confuses its speech and
authority with the language-norms and authorities of alien systems
of thought and communities of language. Theology is the attempt
by the Church to discover above this confusion its own norms and
thus its essential language-criteria. As Karl Barth puts it,

> Theology follows the language of the Church, so far as, in its questions
> as to the correctness of the Church's procedure therein, it measures it,
> not by a standard foreign to her, but by her very own source and object.
> Theology guides the language of the Church, so far as it concretely re-
> minds her that in all circumstances it is fallible human work, which in
> the matter of relevance or irrelevance lies in the balance, and must be
> obedient to grace, if it is to be well done. Theology accompanies the
> language of the Church, so far as it is itself nothing but human "language
> about God," so far as, with that language, it stands under the judgment
> that begins with the house of God, and so far as, with it, it lives by the
> promise given to the Church.[15]

In this task of systematic theology the intimate relations become
apparent between the language of the Church and the Word of
God in the Bible and (above all) in Jesus Christ. The Church finds
the Word as event by faithfully attending to the Word of the Bible
and is thereby constituted as the Church of Christ (the Body of
Christ), finding the ultimate standard for its language in Jesus.
"The criterion of Christian language, in past and future as well
as at the present time, is thus the essence of the Church, which is
Jesus Christ, God in his gracious approach to man in revelation
and reconciliation. Has Christian language its source in Him? Does
it lead to Him? Does it conform to Him?"[16] It will only be by the
logic of faithful obedience to the Analogy of Christ, it is said, that
theological language can be tested for adequacy. Only the Church
which honors Scripture and finds through its inspired pages immediate acquaintance with Christ, the living Word, will be able to
test its language with "true objectivity." Such wider "objectivity"
is a prerequisite for the vital task of recasting the language of
theology in each generation.

This can be accomplished only by having constant recourse to the
living Word. It is in listening here that the Church will be able to mint
out of broken human language and antiquated categories the new coinage

which may convey more effectively to a needy world the unspeakable riches of Christ.[17]

True as it is, on the logic of obedience, that the ultimate justification for the language of the Church is the supernatural gift of God's Word and that, in consequence, the characteristic posture of the obedient fellowship must be one of "listening" in faith for this Word, it should not be concluded from this that the theology of obedience advocates quietism or the cultivation of "voices." On the contrary, "listening" should never be taken to suggest the static picture of a hand poised at an ear; there is no place for such scenes of suspended animation in the obedient "listening" of the Church. The Church is prepared to "listen" only when it is *in act* —worshiping, serving, exemplifying Christ in contemporary history. Someone, perhaps, might suggest that at least the Church's *first* responsibility is to test its language of proclamation against certain theological criteria and *then,* when the dogmatic core of her message is secured, to "translate" those theological findings into appropriate action. But this order of procedure is precisely the order which is impossible for obedience! Only in the context of the total life of the Church can theology function, as we have recently noted; but such total life must include the ongoing activities—in every sphere—by which the Church expresses its obedience. Therefore theological criticism cannot rule over the activities of the Church since these activities are a necessary condition of theology's very existence. Not only is theology incapable of dominating the concrete activity of the Church in practice, but even in principle the suggestion that language is supreme over action violates biblical authority. The Reverend Dr. Ian Fraser, who differs theologically in important respects from theologians of obedience like Professor Torrance, none the less reminds us:

We find no justification in the Bible for the belief that sound doctrine can be hammered out in abstraction from spheres of obedience. Instead we are told: "If any man will do His will, he shall know of the doctrine."[18]

Such "doing" must include both acts of worship and the works of *agape* which are implicit in the Christian's obligation. The theologian, like the simplest believer, cannot afford to neglect either element in this dual demand; the first is the source of theology and the second sustains it. As Fraser says, "Theology draws its very life from worship, and in that life draws its nourishment from obedience."[19] The theologian must face his task as a "fully human" (that is, active) figure, because he cannot successfully carry out his job if he neglects what is an essential condition for his work.

The theologian, though the nature of his function makes it necessary that he abstract himself from his full humanity in order to pursue an intellectual activity, must yet speak *from* his full redeemed humanity if he is to declare any λόγος τοῦ Θεοῦ. He must speak not only *qua* technical expert, but also *qua* obedient man if he is to speak theological sense.[20]

The language of Christianity is dependent, therefore, on the Church's "listening" from the turbulent center of its own full life, and such speech derives from the same supernatural impulse which stirs the Church to other, non-verbal, forms of expression. But far from dictating to the Church the form its life shall take, theological language is the follower of obedient action, not its leader. Action, Fraser tells us, is intimately related to doctrinal language, "but it is not under final authority except to God Himself, in His unique right to call men to any form of response to Him in this world."[21]

Thus in times like those of the ancient prophets, when God calls men to rapidly changing forms of active obedience, the linguistic formulae of theology are likely to be left behind by the pace of events. For this reason

. . . it should not be asked of present prophetic movements that their character should form a picture to fit any present theological frame. Such movements, wherever they are found, will provide material for new theological systems: and may remind us of the essentially fragmentary nature of any such systems.[22]

The most characteristic language of the Church, the language of preaching, must, according to the logic of obedience, be understood in the foregoing terms. Once more we find the Analogy of Christ and of "incarnation." On one level, in the preaching-situation, we discover the human preacher uttering his human words—of greater or less wisdom and helpfulness—to a group of people listening with varying degrees of profit to a homily based on some scriptural passage. But out of this lower-level state of affairs can rise, by the miraculous inspiration of God, a higher-level event which is none other than the proclamation of the Word of God. All three lower-level elements, the preacher, the people, and the Bible, must be present as a "form" ready for God to fill, but none of them alone or even all together can proclaim the Word of authority in their own power. Some Protestants have implied, Daniel Jenkins says, that the Word of God is spoken simply through the minister, but this is a serious mistake. The Word, in fact,

. . . is spoken by God in the waiting upon Him of the congregation, in the encounter between His Word in Scripture and the real situation of that particular group of people. The minister performs an essential function in this, but it is only one function among others. His task is to help the congregation to reach the place where they can hear God speaking for themselves, by providing the necessary means for their understanding what the Scriptures are saying and what the light of tradition as a whole is for their present situation. . . . Both minister and people are meant to have Scripture before them and both are conscious of standing in the living tradition of the Church. The minister has the dialectical task of so speaking that men hear, not him, but the voice of the living God.[23]

No divorce is possible between the worshiping Church and the preacher, and no separation is possible between the preacher and the Holy Scriptures if the words of preaching are to become God's Word. The preacher can never be sure that his language is God's, and therefore never is himself beyond the need for obedience in faith—he has no excuse for spiritual pride or self-righteousness or fanaticism—but he can and must preach in faith and hope that the miracles of the past, when God made imperfect human language his own divine instrument, will be repeated for his congregation.

The task of the preacher of the Word is to expound the scripture in the midst of the worshipping Church, preaching in the expectancy that God will do, through his frail human word, what He did through the Word of His prophets of old, that God by His grace will cause the word that goes out of the mouth of man to become also a Word that proceeds from God Himself, with all the power and efficacy of the Word of the Creator and Redeemer. The word preached by man can become "God speaking."[24]

Theological discourse is not valued by the logic of obedience, then, for any philosophical insights it may offer, for its intrinsic wisdom, for any profound meaningfulness it possesses—even for any intrinsic truth it may claim as its own. Supporters of the logic of obedience seem to go to great lengths to stress the intrinsic incapability of theological discourse to speak meaningfully and truly about God. "The words of the preacher, however well chosen, however cleverly arranged, however eloquently spoken, fall short of their object," insists G. S. Hendry, "for they are, in the last resort, attempts to express what no words of man can express, the authentic Word of God which is living and powerful and sharper than any two-edged sword."[25] Only the gift of God's enlightening Spirit can bring meaning and truth out of meaninglessness and falsehood. It is this divine gift, not any human decision to "believe" or "have faith," which makes possible the obedience on which theological truth and meaning depend. True faith is not a human possibility. The corruption of mankind by sin is too complete to allow a natural capacity for God's truth, even by obedience, if that obedience is the arbitrary choice of the believing subject. In the logic of obedience, as N. H. G. Robinson puts it, "there is no room for the believer's exaltation of the facts of revelation over other facts. Such a representation of the matter in fact exalts the believer and puts the self-revelation of God at the disposal of man's mind as a mere object."[26]

How then is the obedience of faith possible? With men it may be impossible, but with God all things are possible. "It is not the believer but God who exalts the name of Jesus Christ far above every other name."[27] The fact is that faith is humanly impossible but that faith does take place. Thus, "faith is not a natural capacity we bring with us to the Word, but a hearing that God gives us in His giving of the Word itself."[28]

If this is the case, as the logic of obedience claims, then faith, and, springing from it, the meaningful character of theological discourse, will not be open to the kinds of analysis to which it is often put. On the level of what Torrance calls "autonomous" or "self-enclosed" reason, the language of theology will always remain mysterious—or, as those lacking the power to be "truly critical" may put it, it must be invalid and nonsensical. But, in the wider sense of "rationality" defined by Torrance, the only really rational policy for logical analysis confronted with mysterious theological language is humbly to suspend judgment and to await the converting and revealing Word "from without."

To suspend judgment is not to be irrational; rather is it the part of reason which behaves obediently in terms of its object, in this instance, an objective Revelation which even in the event of revelation remains a *mysterion*, and will not yield its secret to analytical and logical investigation.[29]

For those who are willing to respond thus "rationally," theological discourse does not cease to present problems; but these problems are no obstacle to God!

We might take these human words of ours in full recognition of the fact that they were in themselves quite inadequate, carry them up, as it were, to God's own revelation of Himself, and allow that revelation to give them a meaning of its own. We might say: these words of ours are, in themselves, quite meaningless as applied to God, but they are the only words we have, and God may use them as a medium to convey to us the truth about Himself. These human words of ours can become charged with new and divine content. While in themselves meaningless they can be made meaningful. Or, better, we shall say that while in themselves they convey positive untruth, they can be so laid hold of by God as to yield real illumination.[30]

III

Despite the intensity of conviction and the uncompromising directness of the logic of obedience, I cannot accept its account as in any way a justification for theological language—although, as I hope to show, this logic throws some indirect light on the nature of theological discourse which may be of use later in constructing a more adequate theory. It is impossible, first, to remain content theologically or philosophically with the divorce which obedience allows—glories in!—between the logical character of human theological discourse and the "meaning" and "truth" which is allegedly "breathed into" it miraculously and independent of its nature. What can possibly be further from a genuinely "incarnational" view than this position of "logical docetism"? The value of the human is minimized, denied, and deplored ostensibly to glorify the miraculous inspiration of the divine; but such a policy can never lead to a genuine theory of incarnation, only to a violation of the debased human by the divine which, instead of "inspiring" the human, assaults and replaces it.

In making the logical structure of theological language thus irrelevant to the content it supposedly bears, obedience not only has violated its own governing Christocentric analogy but also has called into question the nature of theological meaning and truth. What possible difference can it make (if "in themselves they convey positive untruth") *which* "positively untruthful" words happen to be spoken by the theologian or preacher? Why, if "these words of ours are, in themselves, quite meaningless as applied to God," are the meaningless words of Scripture more to be respected than the meaningless words of a racing tabloid? If it is answered that God might make use of the lists of the starters at Epsom Downs to convey his Word with the same ease and likelihood as the Gospel of John, we must ask why the Church treasures Scripture in a way it fails to treasure stock-market reports, racing forms, scandal sheets, and so on. If it is countered that God happens, as a rule, to choose language with certain logical characteristics and subject matter through which to reveal himself, we must conclude that the nature of the human language is not, after all, without relevance. What is it, then, that distinguishes the "false or nonsensical language" which God happens to choose as appropriate for his "miraculous inspiration" from all other forms of false or nonsensical language—or, indeed, from the sheerest babbling or the boldest lie? Or is God's alleged "election" of the language of the Bible and the Church no more than an arbitrary whim?

Aside from this question, however, and granting that the words of the Church's Scripture and preaching sometimes strike fire as "God's truth" and sometimes remain "mere words," what implication does this have for the nature of theological significance? Language which is meaningless at one moment suddenly impresses its hearer or reader with its "meaning." This phenomenon has two parallels in ordinary (drug-free) experience which may fully account for the theological instance. First, one sometimes makes a sudden discovery of the point of a metaphor, when what had not "made sense" before all at once "rings a bell." Ian Ramsey refers to this kind of experience in *Religious Language* where he speaks of "the penny dropping" and sudden comprehension flooding the mind. Second, the sense of being "uplifted," as by great poetry or music, is not uncommon. Here the literal content expressed may be of little importance or missing altogether, as in music, but the sense of meaning and of importance may be strongly felt as an objective fact "from without." Ronald Hepburn, in his analysis of such experience, finds in the notion of importance a key to the understanding of the claim that literally meaningless discourse suddenly becomes lifted into meaningfulness. This feeling of cognitive meaningfulness is an illusion, but it is an illusion that "may be necessary to maintaining the sense of momentousness"[31] which the experience does undoubtedly possess. For the logic of obedience to stress this side of theological language while maintaining its logical worthlessness is to discard "significance" for theological discourse in the sense of *meaning* and to substitute for it "significance" in the sense of *importance* only.

But what of the "truth" which is supposedly given "from without" by God's miraculous gift of his Word? Meaning is a logical prerequisite for truth or for falsity. That which has *no* sense cannot have a *true* sense. Is it objected that this is so only on the basis of "philosophical reason" and as such is irrelevant to the truth from beyond the self-enclosed canons of autonomous reason? Then what is meant by this "supreme truth"? Is it an empty concept? Then we may disregard it. Is it thinkable? Then it is irresponsible of the logic of obedience to urge us to refrain from employing the only reliable tests available to us for the sake of vindicating it, if possible, and of distinguishing it from all pretenders.

The crucial claim made by Torrance in his valiant attempt to redefine "critical reason" in order not to be forced openly to abandon the term (as well as the reality) is that there is at least one "object" to which the criteria and techniques of normal rationality ought not to be applied. This "object" is identified as the experience of meaningfulness and truth which Torrance calls the Word of God, and it defies normal reason because it is not of the same order as human mentality but comes to man "from without." Philosophers, with their canons of ordinary rationality, are no doubt supposed to refrain even from examining this *claim,* on which all depends, that the experience is in fact an ingression from a supernatural realm of being, meaning, and truth. Then the logic of obedience would be safe and the main questions of the philosophy of religion neatly avoided. But it would be the height of irresponsibility for anyone more concerned for impartial truth than for the defense of a party line to shrug off a challenge like that offered by the logic of obedience to independent criticism. Many experiences possess the characteristic of intentionality, of coming "from without." Among them are "introspective" experiences, which seem to their experiencers to be of overwhelming importance. Jung and his followers deal with such experience when they hypothesize archetypal images from the racial unconscious "entering" the field of inner perception. Such talk from Jung, which *"externalizes* the unconscious, and suggests strongly that we are 'visited' from something not ourselves when the archetypes are present to us," is a "dramatic metaphor," as Hepburn puts it, "constantly on the point of begging the question."[32] Theologians are equally vulnerable to this charge.

Even if there were to be grounds for supposing that the Word of God is genuinely "from without" and if we were ready, in consequence, to allow Torrance to place this Word beyond possibility of ordinary rational criticism, what possible right would we or anyone—including Torrance—have then to reject any and every claim to special dispensation for his own "Word"? Only by applying the sort of criteria which Torrance rejects as inapplicable could the floodgates be closed against the endless absurdities of innumerable fanatics and the weird lunacies of the deranged or the irresponsible. H. J. Paton rightly warns the defenders of the logic of obedience: "To declare war upon reason is to alienate all who care for truth and to hold open the door for the imposter and the zealot."[33]

"Who is man," the logic of obedience asks, "to sit in judgment on the Word of God?" We are *judged* by obedience or lack of it before the Word; we do not rightly judge it. Even to raise such questions as we have here is proof of pride and the alienation of the questioner from God. This, after all, is the last word which obedience knows how to speak. But denunciation as a weapon cuts both ways. We may turn this final blow, as Paton deftly does, by noting that "a very little modesty might suggest to the prophet that to question the truth of his message is not the same thing as to sit in judgement upon God. Theological arrogance can also be a form of sinful pride."[34]

What, if anything, may be salvaged from this theological tradition despite its serious defectiveness? I am convinced that the emphasis placed by the logic of obedience on the role of the Church and the Bible in the molding of theological discourse is both valid and of considerable importance. Despite obscurantist protestations to the contrary, the logic of obedience does provide for criteria by which human theological discourse may be interpreted. Primary among these criteria is Scripture, the language of which is taken as authoritative by the language-using community of the Church. The Bible, in the logic of obedience, serves much the same function that analogical rules serve within the logic of analogy; this function is to license the use of certain linguistic formulae and to ban the use of others. Compatibility with the language of the Bible (discovered, by the way, through the skillful use of the techniques of "autonomous reason") is one necessary condition for permissible Christian talk about God. The logic of obedience, in directing attention to the Bible, offers an authoritative standard on the syntactical level of theological discourse for the Christian religion. A fully developed theory of theological discourse might well generalize on the basis of this hint and search for similar authoritative language-standards in other religions. The intriguing complexities of this syntactical dimension of theological discourse have yet to be fully explored by interested philosophers.

The emphasis of the logic of obedience on the Church, on the other hand, reminds us that, if language is always social, syntactical usage is always within a linguistic community. Beyond this, obedience is correct in insisting that any community of human beings will be engaged in more than talk alone. The Church as actor is the ground for, and occasion of, theological discourse. Only in terms of its interpreters and its users will theological discourse be adequately understood. We are reminded of the basic tenet of functional analysis that one must look for the meaning of any language in a social context where it has a genuine use. For theological language the Church provides this context. The logic of obedience has correctly emphasized its vital role.

8

THE LOGIC OF ENCOUNTER

WE MUST now deal with the approach to theological discourse which will be the most familiar one to a large number of readers. Thus far we have noticed the place of "religious experience" only in passing. The logic of analogy claims no need for such experience. The logic of obedience refuses, in theory at least, to admit its dependence on any "merely human" experience; it insists that faith is not an "experience" but a divine imperative which judges and transforms all of man's sin-ridden experiences. The third theological tradition concerning the language of theism, in contrast, openly regards an experience called "encounter with God" as central to the understanding of theological speech. This logic of encounter, indeed, holds that without its experiential foundation theological discourse would be devoid of meaning and irrelevant to truth-claims.

I

At the outset the supporters of this logic are required to defend themselves against the accusation that in choosing the term "encounter" they have begged the question of the objective reference of theism. The most straightforward reply from the logic of encounter to this charge will admit the question-begging but insist that the circumstances admit no alternative. "Encounter" refers to the experience of those moments when the self finds itself so manifestly confronted by another, independent "Thou" that objective reference is part of the datum. The sense of communion is so close and the feeling of reality so overwhelming that to choose language describing it which admitted even the possibility of separating experience from objective ground of experience would be to distort the unique and "self-verifying" nature of experience itself.

The best language to express the experience, therefore, is language which analytically entails an independent "Thou" to be "encountered." As Professor E. P. Dickie states it, the conviction following the experience of encounter is "conviction which arises *from the coercive element in reality*. We believe because we must, and we also believe that the coercion comes from God."[1]

Thus a *petitio principii* is in fact involved in the terminology of the logic of encounter, but such a *petitio* is the only logically appropriate way of bringing out the nature of the conviction with which the logic of encounter is concerned. This conviction is "beyond question"—not, as for the logic of obedience, in the sense that questions may not be *raised* by those who do not themselves know what it is to "encounter God," but in the sense that any *answer* to these questions in terms other than those rooted in the "encounter" itself would be logically inappropriate—and so the quality of the conviction is best expressed by the frank employment of a question-begging term.

II

H. H. Farmer, in his recent Gifford Lectures, analyzes the meaning of "God" and, more precisely, the meaning of Christian language expressing the puzzling doctrine of the Trinity, in terms of the logic of encounter. The experience which lies at the logical root of Trinitarian theological language takes place supremely in Christian worship, Farmer states; thus those interested in understanding this language must not shy away from the method of "productive empathy." He himself adopts the procedure wherein "we frankly begin from within the sphere of Christian religious experience in which we ourselves, as Christian philosophers of religion, share at first hand."[2]

The worshiping Christian finds a concretely Trinitarian God in his encounter-experience. Only in terms of God the "Father," "Son," and "Holy Spirit" does the encounter find relatively adequate expression in language. But even this expression is ultimately inadequate owing to the "otherness" which is part of the encounter and which therefore resists all classification. "The Christian in his worship is aware of being in relation to a reality which is *sui generis,* essentially and radically different from any other kind of reality with which it is possible to be in relation."[3] Thus:

> Whatever we may try to say in explication of . . . the term "God," something vital must in the nature of the case be left unexpressed; and what must be omitted is precisely that which, if it were subtracted from the act of worship, would make is cease to be the worship of *God.*[4]

The encounter, we find, is with the "other," but, despite the "otherness" of the "Thou" encountered, the "veritably personal"[5] character of the Thou *is part of the experience,* thus legitimating the use of the personal term "Father" in reference to God. Again, we meet a personality which is both warm and stern ("both giving all and demanding all," in Farmer's terms) and we recognize in this encounter the "Son," who requires absolute discipleship but who gave himself on a cross for all men. In contrast—but as an integral part of the same encounter-experience—we are aware of an element which penetrates beneath the level of discrete personality (as in the "Father" and "Son") to unite with our own sub-personal depths. This we call the "Holy Spirit." There may, perhaps, be a *theoretical* problem of reconciling the personal and the non-personal when we consider theological language apart from the encounter-experience which gives it rise, but in the *experiences* of worship

> . . . the two things—the "I-thou" relation to God and the divine indwelling—are not set in opposition to one another but are rather held together in a way that is deeply and characteristically Christian and in which there is not felt to be, so far as the living apprehension of God in worship is concerned, any problem at all.[6]

Given personal encounter with God, the meaning of our language about him presents no insurmountable problem; without such encounter, no amount of talk will provide it with genuine significance.

The fact that theological discourse employs such words as "Father" and "Son" to refer to the encounter which undergirds its meaning makes it clear that the logic of encounter does not attempt to avoid use of symbols widely removed from their literal contexts. This provides both drawbacks and advantages for supporters of this logic. An advantage is found in the flexibility which the position makes possible; the theologian can go to the philosophical critic with a happy combination of humility and confidence: unshakable confidence in the reality he has encountered and genuine humility concerning his efforts at symbolizing that reality. He may say to the philosopher, as W. S. Urquhart suggests:

"Here are our conclusions, the results of our total-response to the Reality with which we have felt ourselves confronted. Examine these conclusions, pull them to pieces if you like, but do not throw them away as negligible. See if you can put them together again better than the theologians have yet done, and be very sure we ourselves do not regard them as final. We shall come back again with fresh formulations. Only the Reality which we all seek to interpret is absolute and final."[7]

Symbols, especially such symbols as cannot in principle be paraphrased in literal terms but only substituted for by other imperfect symbols, may not satisfy the person who is normally content only with literal scientific discourse. But, urges the logic of encounter, he must shape his expectations to the nature of the subject matter. And, most important, through the choice of the *right* symbols (testing them against moments of encounter experienced in the past) he will be able to meet in immediate experience again and again the One about whom literal language drawn from finite experience cannot speak.

Only at one point do theologians of encounter often draw the line fast against symbolism. One experience, one word referring to a quality found in encounter, is non-symbolic. The literal term is "love." When the Thou of our heavenly Father meets us in intimate communion, we experience the same all-giving, all-winning force which we meet in the very highest of our human relations. Dean Inge says,

. . . when we say that God is Love we make this affirmation not merely "analogically" but directly. In other words, love as we know it differs from divine love in degree, but not in kind.[8]

And Professor Edgar P. Dickie agrees: "The love which man experiences for God Who has created and redeemed him is not something alien to the divine nature; but, in the providence and mercy of God, is of the same texture."[9] It is in this experience of the highest love, which is a gift from God to man, that we break through the veil of symbol and at this one point speak of the

"Thou" of our encounter as he literally is. We have no need of more.

The disadvantages, recognized by the logic of encounter, which are associated with highly symbolic speech are imprecision and paradox. Neither seems to be avoidable, but both, according to the logic of encounter, are mitigated by a proper understanding of the basic function of theological discourse. This function is to point hearer and speaker alike back to the experiential source in which it is rooted. Theological language, we are told, is ultimately justifiable only as a means to the end of obtaining religious experience. Thus the imprecision of theological symbols is forgotten once the encounter from which it springs and to which it leads is experienced in its inexpressible immediateness. In like manner, verbal paradoxes due to the clash of symbols will be interpreted. More, thanks to the logic of encounter (it is claimed), a criterion may be provided whereby legitimate paradox may be distinguished from what Ronald Hepburn in *Christianity and Paradox* calls "viciously muddled confusion of concepts."[10]

The late Professor D. M. Baillie discusses paradox at some length in *God Was in Christ* and names one fundamental cause of the appearance of verbally contradictory statements in theology:

> The reason why the element of paradox comes into all religious thought and statement is because God cannot be comprehended in any human words or in any of the categories of our finite thought. God can be known only in a direct personal relationship, an "I-and-Thou" intercourse, in which He addresses us and we respond to Him.[11]

Our words, we have repeatedly discovered, have been devised for other jobs than for expressing literal truths about God; *any* words, in fact, will be inadequate because of their inherent tendency to objectify and to classify whatever they denote. God, we are warned not to forget, is a spiritual Subject, never a mere object; God is unique, never classifiable. Therefore, "He eludes all our words and categories. We cannot objectify or conceptualize Him. When we try, we fall immediately into contradiction."[12]

Baillie deflates the unwarranted aura of mystery which clings to theological paradox by comparing contradictions between incompatible theological statements with the "contradictions" between different two-dimensional map projections of our spherical earth.

Such projections distort the reality which they attempt to symbolize even as they succeed in referring usefully to it, because although the reality is a *sphere* they offer us only marks in a *plane*. But different projections distort the reality differently; a polar projection (taken by itself) must "contradict" a Mercator projection (also taken by itself).

They would be either misleading or mystifying to anyone who did not know that they represent the surface of a sphere. But they can serve their useful purpose for anyone who understands that they are intended simply to represent in handy portable form the pattern covering the surface of this round earth which he knows in actual experience. So it is with the paradoxes of faith. They are inevitable, not because the divine reality is self-contradictory, but because when we "objectify" it all our judgments are in some measure falsified, and the higher truth which reconciles them cannot be fully expressed in words, though it is experienced and lived in the "I-and-Thou" relationship of faith towards God.[13]

This theory of the source of paradoxes provides us at the same time with a criterion with which to select the legitimate paradoxes and reject the mere contradictions generated by confused or lazy thinking. Just as projections of the world can be mistaken, and are shown to be so by ultimate reference to the experienced earth itself, so theological paradoxes must be tested by reference back to the experience of encounter which is their ultimate justification—or condemnation.

There should always be a sense of tension between the two opposite sides of our paradoxes, driving us back to their source in our actual religious experience or faith. That is where we must refine our theological statements, purging them of needless contradictions and testing them "whether they be of God." Thus no paradox in theology can be justified unless it can be shown to spring directly from what H. R. Mackintosh called "the immediate utterances of faith"; for since a paradox is a self-contradictory statement, we simply *do not know what it means or what we mean by it* unless it has that direct connection with the faith which it attempts to express.[14]

Although the logic of encounter emphasizes the source of the meaning of theological language in individual experience, this logic is not individualistic. True, it is said

. . . God makes Himself known to man by encountering him as an abso-

lute claim upon his will and as the final succour and security of his life. It
is therefore only as a self-conscious individual, only as he is conscious in
some way, however crude and dim, . . . that man can be religious at
all.[15]

But the essential sociality of language, including theological language, is recognized by the logic of encounter through its appre-
ciative view of Church and Scripture in their respective roles. The
Bible, and the language which composes it, is itself a product of
encounter, a record of encounter, and a perpetuator of encounter
for each generation. "Public revelation" through Scripture cannot
be thought to be logically independent of the "private" religious
experience of those who wrote the words which, through their supreme aptness to the encounter-experience and through their un-
rivaled ability to lead others to fresh experience, are today
authoritative. "In fact . . . public revelation itself must be the religious experience of the revealers, be they prophets, apostles or
Jesus Christ."[16]

The Bible, for the logic of encounter, was written because men
experienced encounter with God in the course of Israel's history.
The Church, too, grew out of the same history of encounters which
forged the Bible, and it lives inseparable from its Scriptures. When
it is true to itself as a Church, the believing community knows that
it does not exist merely to perpetuate itself but for the sake of the
God who encounters its members in worship and there stimulates
them to speak the language of faith and to act the life of reconciliation and love.

III

The emphasis provided by the logic of encounter on the importance of personal experience for all language, including theological language, is welcome; but two serious shortcomings prevent
us from finding in the logic of encounter a fully adequate interpretation and defense for the meaningfulness of theological discourse. The notion of "encounter" which is at the root of this
position is beset with difficulties, and the theory of "testing"
symbols against religious experience leads to what, for the theist,
are unfortunate consequences.

Turning first to the problem of testing symbols against encounter, we must ask what the real measure of "appropriateness" of a

symbol to the experience can be. No external standard is ultimately capable of arbitrating on this matter; even the Bible serves as authority only because its words are adjudged "appropriate" to the experience of each generation of readers. The writers of the Bible must themselves have had to determine the "appropriateness" of their words to the encounter-experience without an external standard on the logic of encounter; or, if they relied on some previous authority (earlier documents, oral tradition), the regression of dependence upon external criteria must end somewhere short of infinity. What, if the final criterion of "appropriateness" between language and encounter-experience must be "internal," is this standard?

C. A. Campbell turned his attention to this question in his St. Andrews University Gifford Lectures. There he identified the criterion for judging the appropriateness of theological symbols as one's "feelings." All language, he points out in the published lectures, is negated as literally applicable to God, but

. . . not all of the negations have for the religious consciousness the same status. *Positive* value-terms—Justice, Love, Mercy and the like—are negated because of their felt inadequacy to God, whose value is transcendent and ineffable; whereas *dis*value terms—Injustice, Hatred, Cruelty and the like—are negated not just because of their felt *inadequacy*, but also, and primarily, because of their felt [sic!] *contrariety*, to the Divine nature. Clearly there is a vital difference between negations which proceed upon such different principles; and it is precisely because there *is* this difference, to which the religious consciousness bears consistent witness, that it makes sense to say that the value-terms, e.g. Justice, Love, and Mercy, though not literally applicable to God, are applicable to him in a "symbolic" significance. Were is not for this felt [sic!] difference of principle within negation, there would be no case for holding that there is even symbolic knowledge about God.[17]

Campbell tries to hold that symbols are allowed or disallowed by "religious consciousness" on the basis of principles, but in fact his "different principles" are nothing other than different *feelings* about terms which are proposed. He even refers, in a following passage, to the vital role of the "emotions aroused" by the symbols in question. Some symbols evoke a feeling of strong "natural affinity," he insists, which the human mind finds itself obliged to accept even while it cannot "understand" it. "It is this that confers on symbols like wisdom, love and justice objectivity and necessity as symbols of the Divine nature. . . ."[18]

But if this is all that justifies the choice of certain symbols to "point back to" and "lead on to" the experience of meeting God according to the logic of encounter, the position as a whole is exceedingly vulnerable. The emotional approval which attaches to certain symbols because of their use in ordinary discourse may be a powerful causal factor in influencing people to employ these terms in theological discourse, but such approval alone is no rational justification. On the contrary, the discovery that symbols in theological language are ultimately judged appropriate or inappropriate on the basis of such feelings would tend to justify a degree of skeptical reserve toward the logic of encounter which permits—no, requires—so notoriously untrustworthy a criterion. It would force us to wonder how far the logic of encounter has in reality advanced beyond the position sardonically put, long ago, into the mouth of Philo by David Hume: "Wisdom, thought, design, knowledge; these we justly ascribe to him [God]; because these words are honourable among men, and we have no other language or other conceptions, by which we can express our adoration of him."[19]

Ronald Hepburn, in respect to the second major shortcoming of the logic of encounter, devotes two chapters of his recent book to a damaging criticism of "encounters" themselves. In describing the "encounter-experience" by means of words like "Thou," Hepburn shows, the "vital analogy . . . is that between meeting people and meeting God." If it were not for this analogy, it is clear, there would be no linguistic ground for affirming the "personality" of the God encountered or for using terms like "Father" or "Son" with reference to him. But, Hepburn asks, "have the theologians established this analogy firmly enough to bear the weighty superstructure that they have reared upon it?"[20] The reply to this question, without doubt, must be in the negative.

In the first place, can the logic of encounter wish to claim that *all* that Christians mean by "God" can be exhausted by reference to certain human experiences? Surely not! Statements about "God" would then be equivalent to statements about human experience, and it would be nonsense—by definition—to speak about "God's existence" prior to the existence of human beings possessing such experiences. The definition of "God" may well be held essentially to include reference to human experiences, but traditional theism will always insist on more than this in any complete definition. And yet the moment that a "more" is required, we are confronted with a metaphysical issue concerning a being who is the independent cause or source of the so-called "encounter-experiences." In this way the logic of encounter subtly slips from an overt attempt at explicating the *meaning* of theological terms to a covert argument to the *existence* of God from religious experience. And if encounter proves both suspiciously subjectivist and logically incomplete as a theory of theological meaningfulness, it exhibits itself equally weak as convincing evidence for the existence of a divine Encounterer.

Even the best examples of the "I-Thou" encounters on which the theological case must rest turn out to be weak reeds. No matter how profound the "rapport," no matter how convincing the experience of genuine "I-Thou" contact between two persons, there is always the possibility—and often the actuality—of a mistake. How disillusioning, after a prolonged period of silent "encounter" with a friend, to have the spell broken by hearing a sudden snore issuing from the other "Thou," who, it turns out, has been sound asleep the whole time! How shattering to discover that someone who has been thoroughly known, it seems, through "encounter" is really quite a different person from the one formerly imagined!

Something John tells me one day about himself, or something I see him do, convinces me that I have never really known his "centre" or his true personality. The kaleidoscope is suddenly reshuffled, a quite *new* "uniqueness" is given to my relation with him. The impression I had formerly had of his personality was a highly particular one, concrete and impossible to generalize about (like all good *I-Thou* instances)—yet in some way it was fraught with illusion.[21]

If illusion is present sometimes or often in "encounter," what assures us that our experience is not *always* merely subjective emotion conjoined with personal interpretation? Even if the rapport between persons is sometimes veridical, as seems increasingly likely in the light of contemporary research into para-normal psychology, it is clear from the negative instances that this route to knowledge of other persons is far from trustworthy, and therefore hardly adequate to undergird the entire theological claim to the knowledge of God.

But a further difficulty within the notion of "encounter" in its theological application arises over the very notion of error in "I-Thou" experiences. How does one discover that he was mistaken in his supposition that he had been "encountered" by the true personality of another? Such mistakes are always discovered by observations of a sort which are out of the question for theological "encounter." Hearing a snore; seeing a covert act, gesture, or facial expression; feeling a stab in the back—these are the means, often painful, of distinguishing sheer illusion from what may conceivably be veridical extra-sensory perception. The logic of encounter, by ruling out any such independent tests (which would be impossible to conceive, it would seem, even if they were desired), has effectively blocked any means of distinguishing between "genuine" encounter with God and the illusory products of supercharged emotions.

The analogy from human "encounters" suggests that at least some of the experiences which are held to be "encounter with God" really are subjectively produced; can the mere claim that the experiences are "self-verifying" rule out the uncomfortable suspicion that, when dissociated from any empirical personality, they all may be only illusion? What, in any case, is the logical status of "self-verifying"? We must turn now to this question and others, never adequately examined by theologians themselves, with the explicit tools of functional analysis. Our decision to attend to the thoughts of theologians themselves concerning their language has provided us with profitable—and indispensable—insights but with no definite resting place.

9

THE "IMPROPER" FUNCTIONS OF THEOLOGICAL DISCOURSE

WE HAVE been following the advice of functional analysis in the last three chapters, inquiring directly of the users of theological language concerning the meaning, purpose, and justification of their discourse. We found three different answers, no one of which satisfied us as stated. This outcome should not surprise us. The primary job of the theologian is not to philosophize about his language but to use it. And, as R. M. Hare puts it,

. . . many of the logical problems raised are not such as can be dealt with by logical amateurs. For this reason some who know very well how to use religious language have not been able to give a very convincing *account* of its use, just as some gardeners can grow very good vegetables without being able to tell us clearly or even correctly how they do it.[1]

Those best qualified to employ theological discourse are not fully at home in the logical analysis of their speech, we discover, while the highly professional logic of verificational analysis, as we found earlier, is not well adapted to the examination of the subtle logic of theological language. If the essential character of theological discourse is to be uncovered, therefore, it seems that the skilled employment of functional analysis will be the required approach. And, in fact, this more flexible, more empirical way of analyzing theological speech has rightfully received considerable attention in recent years. Some who have used the technique have done so in hopes of discovering what fundamental misuse lurks behind and disqualifies theological discourse; others offer their analyses to show that theological speech serves uncontroversially important functions; still others attempt to distinguish a unique use and thus a distinctive "theological logic" as interpretation—and justification—for theological language. What reasons may be given, first, to show that the theological employment of language is a misuse of speech?

I

C. B. Martin, a philosopher who is far from sure that theological language has any legitimate function, tries to expose further the problems which we have already seen to be associated with the logic of encounter. He remarks on the fact that, as we have seen, many theists intend to make analytically necessary the movement from "experience" to "encounter"—thus from "experience of God" to "objective existence of God." "The assertion 'I have direct experience of God' includes the assertion 'God exists,' " Martin notes; "thus, the conclusion 'therefore, God exists,' follows tautologically."[2]

But when the theist is informed that neither deductive nor inductive support is available for his claim and that introspective experience alone, lacking any public testing procedures, *never* "proves" existence, his response is not to withdraw his claim but to counter with a further assertion that the encounter-experience is "self-verifying"; that is, he holds, *this one* kind of experience is capable of providing a foundation for ontological claims despite the lack of predictive power or testing procedures that are usually required for vindicating an existential claim. Moreover, when the critic asks the theist to specify in some detail what this extraordinary experience is like, the required information is not forthcoming. In addition to being "self-verifying," the theist says, religious experience is also "unique" and thus "incommunicable." Logical analysis is here confronted with a double challenge: to unravel the use of terms like "incommunicable" and *"sui generis"* when used to refer to religious experience, and to analyze the logical functioning of "self-verifying" when used to describe "encounter with God."

Verificational analysis, Martin recognizes, would give short shrift to these terms. A "self-verifying experience" would be dismissed as an absurdity: propositions, not experiences, are subject to verification—and then only by means of public testing procedures which the theist admits are lacking in his case. The claim for "incommunicability," too, would be treated contemptuously. If the theist dares to specify in detail the nature of the experience which allegedly reveals God's existence to the experiencer, he opens the way for falsification: that is, it becomes possible that certain people will have had precisely such experiences as he describes and yet have refused to draw the theist's conclusion. Thus it is in the interest of the theist to assert that to have *these* experiences is to be indubitably confronted with God, and that, in consequence, "You *couldn't* have those experiences and at the same time sincerely deny God's existence."[3] But by so doing the believer has made his claim a purely analytic one, revealing the specialized sense in which he has determined to use his terms but failing to prove that his words have any relevance to existence.

Martin, however, is not content with so summary a dismissal of these theological claims. If they are to be dismissed, it should only be after opportunity is provided theists to defend the claim that this language has a unique logic. Theologians, when thus challenged, say that the logic of the "incommunicability" of religious experience is illuminated by comparisons with the "incommunicability" of color-experience. Just as a color can be known only in the experiencing of it, they say, and just as this first-hand knowledge can never be communicated by mere talk to persons (like those born blind) who have never undergone the experience, so encounter with God must be known immediately to be known at all. Critics who are "God-blind" should no more attack an experience which they cannot imagine than should persons who are totally color-blind ridicule as nonsensical talk about colors. But in offering this plausible explanation of the logic of "incommunicable," Martin thinks, the theist inadvertently exposes to the technique of significant comparison the real logic of his words.

Martin inquires first into the real use which "incommunicable" statements have in both color-language and theological language. In both cases, he concludes, "incommunicable" has the same job: merely to express the inability of one type of experience to be described in terms of another type of experience.

All that this ["incommunicability"] proves is that a description of one group of sensations A in terms of another set of sensations B is never sufficient for knowing group A. According to this definition of "know," in order to know one must have those sensations. Thus, all that is proved is that in order to know what religious experience is one must have a religious experience. This helps in no way at all to prove that such experience is direct apprehension of God and helps in no way to support the existential claim "God exists."[4]

Such an analysis of the function of "incommunicability-language," moreover, shows that any comparison of religious experience with the "incommunicable" or *"sui generis"* experiences of color actually threatens the claim of theological language to deal with more than subjective experience. But, someone objects, my experiences of color certainly have existential implications! True, Martin replies, but whenever we begin to discuss color as a *fact in the world of existence* beyond private "seemings" to see, we bring in a number of methods of verification which make discussion on this level quite different in kind from the sort of discourse which theologians can allow.

If "knowing colour" is to be shaken loose from its purely psychological implications and made to have an existential reference concerning certain features of the world then a whole society of tests and check-up procedures which would be wholly irrelevant to the support of the psychological claim about one's own colour sensations become relevant. E.g. what other people see and the existence of light waves and the description of their characteristics needing the testimony of research workers and scientific instruments.[5]

The theologian is in the uncomfortable position of being able to cling to what at first seemed to be a hopeful analogy of the incommunicability (and importance) of the experience of God with the incommunicability of experiences of color only by endangering the very existential claim with which he begins.

Because "having direct experience of God" does not admit the relevance of a society of tests and checking procedures it places itself in the company of the other ways of knowing which preserve their self-sufficiency, "uniqueness" and "incommunicability" by making a psychological and not an existential claim.[6]

The theologian, Martin insists, should not expect his language to share in the benefits of empirical language without shouldering any of the concomitant responsibility! His "refuge" in claims that his language is *"sui generis"* is "a perfect refuge because no one can prove him wrong, but its unassailability has been bought at the price of making no claim about the world beyond the claim about his own state of mind."[7]

What of the theist's second assertion: that the confrontation of the mind with God is "self-verifying" or "carries its own guarantee"? Functional analysis must probe the real use which this statement has in order to discover its logical force. Is the "inner guarantee" some form of test whose possibility had escaped our notice? No, none is offered. Perhaps, Martin suggests, the real logic behind this language may be revealed by an example which may be taken as a paradigm case of the use of "self-verifying": If all men but one refused to draw the conclusion that religious experience by itself "proves" the existence of God, the last man, if he truly finds in his experience the "guarantee" of his beliefs, would still (on this example) be psychologically able to cling firmly to his assertion.

But if this is the essential meaning of "an experience which carries its own guarantee," then, Martin points out, it has no reference to anything beyond mental and subjective fact. We are left to conclude that "in this matter his experience may be all that ultimately counts for him in establishing his confidence in the truth of his claim about the existence of God."[8] Thus once more, when the theologian's claim is analyzed in terms of its logical functions, we find that it has relevance to "confidence," and "ability to keep on believing," and like uses rather than to matters of fact about existing realities.

It may be worth while at this point to press Martin's analysis somewhat further with the techniques which he himself employs in order to clarify the critique he has launched. We have seen how fundamental to Martin's position the claim is that "merely psychological" experience must be irrelevant to "existence." Let us examine the concept of "existence" as it is used in Martin's argument.

Can we distinguish the paradigm for the use of "existence" which Martin seems to have in mind here? It is evident that any such paradigm will be found among assertions for which "a whole society of tests and check-up procedures" is relevant. Thus for Martin the claim "My experience of yellow in connection with that book is relevant to *existing* realities despite its incommunicability" will be veridical if and only if the assertion is open in principle to testing procedures.

The meaning of "existence," for Martin, is then intimately dependent on what is meant by "testing procedures." Can we be more specific? Yes. Martin tells us that the check-up procedures he has in mind are listening to the testimony of other people, reading the reports of research workers, and examining scientific instruments. "Testing procedures," for Martin, are sense-observations made by independent observers. Now we find that the paradigm for the meaning of the word "existence" which is tacitly employed in this argument is "thing open to relevant sense-observations." Thus for Martin the phrase "existent reality" entails, by definition, "open to test by sense-observation." When it is discovered that theological claims are not so open to test, Martin is able to conclude, by *modus tollens,* that these claims are not about "existent realities" (so defined).

It is not our purpose to enter into a metaphysical discussion of the merits and demerits of this conception of existence, but our understanding of Martin's position is clarified if we see that it *is* based on a theory as to what necessary characteristic any existing being *qua* existing being must possess. This is clearly a metaphysical view on anyone's definition of metaphysics. And equally clearly it is *not* one shared by theists, who, of course, want to say that at least one existing being (God) is not of a nature such that sense-observations could be used as the "testing procedures" which are relevant to check claims about this being.

It now becomes obvious that Martin's analysis is not in itself capable of settling the question of the validity of this "religious way of knowing." His criticism succeeds in posing important issues which, on further probing, are seen to concern the nature of "existence"; but a metaphysical discussion of some kind would be needed to settle the vast questions which are here raised. W. D. Glasgow, replying to Martin, is correct in holding that for the logic of encounter "it is essential . . . for the defender of the religious way of knowing to assert that there are cases where a man *knows* himself to be experiencing an objective Deity. . . ."[9] But Glasgow is misled if he supposes that such "assertion" alone will convince any critics. An analysis of *how* metaphysical statements are cognitive, if they are, will be of more use than mere insistence. I shall return to this point in the final chapter.

Martin's analysis of the function of "self-guaranteeing experience" is also in need of supplementing. He has uncovered only one of at least two functions performed by such locutions, and he has apparently failed to appreciate much of the significance of the one function he did notice.

The one use of the phrase "self-guaranteeing" which he does recognize, we recall, is that of indicating the character of religious experience to be so striking as to convince at least some men of the existence of God *despite anything*. Martin concludes that this function only underscores the "psychological" character of "encounter" —and he is correct as far as he goes. What needs further emphasis, however, is that experience of so striking a character—experience which can be a sufficient condition for belief against all odds and which has supported continued faith in God despite the most ingenious tortures—is experience of a most impressive kind which may, indeed, deserve to be called "unique." It is due, at least, far more careful study than Martin seems to propose by his casual classification of it as "merely psychological." Perhaps this experience will some day be able to be explained with complete adequacy in terms of "conditioning" or the "subconscious" or "glands," but, whether this is the case or not, a proper understanding of experience which is "self-verifying" will be of the greatest interest and importance for an adequate understanding of human life—and, in particular, its religious manifestations.

But calling an experience "self-verifying" has at least one additional logical function. If theology rejects the view that "God" is a physical-object word, the attempt to verify statements about God in the same way that statements about physical objects are verified will seem to theism to be radically mistaken. The statement concerning an "encounter with God" that it "guarantees itself," therefore, is used to warn against possible expectations of logically inappropriate kinds of "guarantees." Such a phrase is used as another way of reminding oneself and others that the "encounter" experience is *ex hypothesi* the only way of relating oneself directly to God; it is to assert with the mnemonic effectiveness of paradox that the only way to "guarantee" the veridical nature of the experience is—to have it!

To recognize this function is not, we must emphasize, to justify the claim that is implicit in the phrase "self-verifying"; but it is to show what use such a phrase may have within the theistic conceptual schema. The effort to justify any fragment of language drawn from that schema, it seems to me, must finally grapple with the justification of the schema as a whole. In like manner, any effective attack on theological language will of necessity be an attack not on isolated fragments of the theist's vocabulary but on the logical tenability of the key concepts which underlie it.

II

Martin directs another of his attacks against precisely these key concepts: at the crucial Christian view of God as perfect goodness and at the logical possibility of the Incarnation.

First, Martin asks how language purporting to affirm the perfect goodness of God functions, logically. It may appear at first glance, when one employs the techniques of significant comparison, that much the same language might be used to refer to a wise and good man, especially since the latter contexts are those which originally give such language a use and thus a meaning. Martin suggests as a paradigm the example of "Father," who is much respected for his moral insight during life and is remembered after his death as completely trustworthy. After Father's death his reputation grows to the stature of infallibility—and there is no longer any chance that future moral lapses on his part will endanger that reputation. Now, Martin asks, is language asserting the goodness (perfect goodness) of Father a good paradigm to illustrate the logical functioning of language asserting God's perfection? Not in the least. The employment of language affirming Father's goodness is based on our evaluation of the moral success of Father's judgments in the past (and could conceivably be disqualified—our language praising his virtue withdrawn—by our finding a secret diary or other evidence showing hypocrisy on his part), but the use of "perfect goodness" language about God is not so based. Quite the contrary; the statement "God is perfectly good" is a tautology based upon the very definition of "God" as "good." But if this is the case, the assertion of the "goodness" of God is analytic and irrelevant to any possible proof or disproof, while the statement "Father was good" is synthetic in form and open to the logical possibility of disproof.

The good is defined in terms of God's will.
God's will (as perfect) is defined in terms of the good.

Nothing in the world of fact or the world of imagination can disturb this equivalence—it rests secure in the cold and barren world of logic. No wonder we found such difference between Father and God.[10]

This analytic use of language, unfortunately, is essential to the theist's position, since to abandon the security of goodness-by-definition would permit as logically possible the (blasphemous) questioning of the perfection of God's goodness. "If God is perfect then nothing *could* count as evidence against his rightness. If anything *could* count as evidence against his rightness then the justification of ethical statements in terms of God's will is not absolute."[11]

His uncovering of the often-unnoticed logical functions of language stating God's goodness rules out, Martin believes, the crucial Christian concept of the Incarnation. The doctrine of the Incarnation, as Martin states it, is that God and Jesus were "one." But, by the very definition of identity, if God and Jesus can be shown to differ in any property (if they are not "indiscernibles"), they cannot be "one." The "goodness" of God, as we have seen, is a goodness-by-definition; the goodness of Jesus, however, is a *judged* goodness, analogous to the goodness of Father. "God" is a concept, separated from the concept "not-good" by conceptual rules; "Jesus" is a proper name possessed by a historical character who can at least in principle be conceived as "not-good." The logical properties of "God" and "Jesus" are so radically different, Martin concludes, that it is sheer absurdity to mumble creeds about their being "one."

Martin is convinced, therefore, that the patient uncovering of the real functions of theological discourse will lead to a clearer understanding of the logical confusions and mistakes which disqualify it. Such an approach via functional analysis will be more effective against theological muddle than the more sweeping program of verificational analysis.

We may agree that Martin's methods represent an advance over the blunter instrument of the verification principle, but I, for one, cannot acquiesce in either his conclusions or his manner of employing these methods. A more careful analysis of the functions of the language which Martin here examines would reveal a basic confusion underlying his entire argument. The same form of words, as we recognized much earlier, can be put to more than one use. The words which make up the sentences "God is good" and "Jesus

Christ was good" may function within kinds of discourse of widely different uses. This fact Martin has failed to notice.

He has seen, it is true, that "God is good" can function in the vocabulary of systematic theology as a definition. This is certainly the case. In systematic language "God is good" functions as a key tautology from which a great many inferences may be drawn. What Martin does not see is that "Jesus Christ was good" may and does also function within the discourse of systematic theology. In that language, it is no less a tautology to state of "the Christ" that he was "good" than to make the same claim about "God." In the systematic language of theology it would be no less a logical contradiction to deny that "the Son" was "good" than to deny "goodness" of "the Father."

What cannot be asserted in the formal language of systematic theology is that "Jesus Christ," the "Son," has *as a matter of historical fact* dwelt among men. In order to anchor the formal conceptual schema of Christian theology to the world of persons and existence the language of living faith, "religious language," is required. In religious discourse (as contrasted with "systematic discourse") it is true, as Martin sees, that "Jesus Christ was good" has a use as a proposition not about a concept but about a historical character whose personal qualities—and very existence—are open to the same judgments of historic probability and disproof as are those of any other. What he fails to notice is that in this language of faith the statement "God is good" *also* functions as a judgment stripped of its analytic invulnerability.

Given a religious rather than a systematic use, the latter statement—which, as we shall see, springs out of an act of commitment and is itself part of the speaker's continuing disposition to commit his life to a theistic model by which to envisage reality—is far from tautological. It is a judgment which both reflects and deeply affects the whole life of the person who utters it in its religious use. The history of religious development and the facts of the religious life illustrate the non-tautological function of "God is good" once this form of words is removed from the systematic language of academic theology. It is all too easy to forget, in our day and culture, that "God" has not always been understood in Christian terms. But it was in fact only after millennia of fear and superstition in which the gods were believed arbitrary, bloodthirsty, and vengeful that the belief in a God of love and goodness gradually entered the world. Such a concept did not arise because philosophers decided to define a term in a certain way; it came, for Western civilization, through the historical experiences of a nation and—supremely for Christians—through the death of a man on a cross.

The main point here is that the notion of "God as good" is a refined concept, forged over the centuries, not "sprung fully armed" from the brow of some thinker. And even today the religious temptation for Christians to doubt the goodness of God is not a logical contradiction, as in Martin's view it would necessarily be. Faith may be sorely tested by great disasters or a personal tragedy. In such circumstances it is not linguistically absurd to say: "Is God good after all? Is his love toward me perfect?" Still less is it an empty tautology to affirm with renewed faith: "Yes, God *is* good! His will *is* perfect!" Thus, for the language of living faith, to affirm that God is good is as much a "judgment" as to assert the goodness of Jesus.

Nothing that has been said here should be taken to minimize the difficulties in the concept of the Incarnation. Kierkegaard may have been right to characterize it as the "supreme absurdity." But Martin's partial analysis, based on a confusion of the logics of two quite different languages, need not add to the theologian's problems. Nor would most theologians accede to Martin's statement of the doctrine. It would be difficult to find an educated Christian who supposes that the Incarnation depends on God and Jesus being "indiscernible" in every respect. Few would seriously be worried by analysts' pointing out, as they occasionally have, that Jesus was in space and time, that he ate, talked, walked, prayed, and so on, and that therefore he logically could not be "one with the Father." If anything at all is agreed by theologians on this central issue it is that God and Jesus have never been supposed (except by heretics) to have been "one" in any sense that these considerations would disturb. The proper sense of "oneness" is the subject of a controversy which does not concern us here. It is, essentially, what arguments about different interpretations of the Incarnation are all about. The interested reader will do well to turn to the vast literature on the subject.[12]

III

Another critique founded on functional analysis is directed by Antony Flew at the language often used by theists to escape the problem of evil. God is supposed by many theists to be exonerated from blame for moral evil if all such evil can be shown to be a logical consequence of God's (blameless) granting to men a genuine measure of freedom. Flew notes that theists claim to find a logical contradiction in the notion that God could grant true human freedom and at the same time *determine* that his creatures never do evil.

If such a logical contradiction can be found, Flew admits, the theist's case is strengthened; but to prove that any logical absurdity prevents one from saying *"free* but wholly *determined* to do good" an analysis of the crucial concept "freedom" is required. Is it the function of the word "free" to rule out, analytically, the use of the word "determined" in the same respect? This is the essential issue, and Flew is convinced that he can prove there is no contradiction

. . . involved in saying that God might have made people so that they always in fact *freely* chose the right. If there is no contradiction here then Omnipotence might have made a world inhabited by wholly virtuous people; the Free-will Defence is broken-backed; and we are back again with the original intractable antinomy.[13]

To make his case Flew self-consciously employs the paradigm case technique. What is the use of the word "free"? Let us provide ourselves with a paradigm of the correct employment of this word, a case, that is, to which we should point in an attempt to *define* the proper use of the word, as follows:

A paradigm case of acting freely, of being free to choose, would be the marriage of two normal young people, when there was no question of the parties "having to get married," and no social or parental pressure on either of them: a case which happily is scarcely rare.[14]

The only evidence which would be relevant to prove the absence of genuine freedom in a standard case like this, Flew holds, would be evidence showing "obstruction or pressure or an absence of alternatives. . . ."[15] The fact that there are *causes* for an action in the personalities and characters of the free agents of this paradigm in no way destroys the *freedom* of the act, so long as there is no external constraint. Good friends often can predict the (free) actions of one another.

And if it is the case that one day a team of psychologists and physiologists will be able to predict a person's behaviour far more completely and successfully than even his best friends now can, even up to one hundred per cent completely and successfully: still this will not show that he never acts freely. . . .[16]

If such an understanding of "freedom," based on this marriage paradigm, is wrong, Flew contends, then human freedom will be able to be fitted into the world only "in the gaps of scientific ignorance"; but this understanding of the use of "freedom" *cannot* be wrong, because a paradigm such as the one employed—including facts about "glands" and "conditioning" with which we must reckon—*are the very originals of the meaning of the language employed,* so that it is by reference to them that the significance of an expression "usually is, and ultimately has always to be, explained."[17] "Free" no more excludes "determined," as logically incompatible, than "solid" excludes "composed of whirling electrical charges." To suppose it does, as theists wish, is to violate the paradigm which gives it meaning.

If complete predictability due to full causal determination is *not* incompatible with freedom (properly understood from the paradigm case), then: "Omnipotence might have, could without contradiction be said to have, created people who would always as a matter of fact freely have chosen to do the right thing."[18] The theologian may no longer hope to excuse an omnipotent God from responsibility for evil on the ground that "freedom" would otherwise be violated, since

. . . if it really is logically possible for an action to be both freely chosen and yet fully determined by caused causes, then the keystone argument of the Free-will Defence, that there is a contradiction in speaking of God so arranging the laws of nature that all men always as a matter of fact freely choose to do the right, cannot hold.[19]

The surface plausibility of the theologian's argument, Flew concludes, was due to the illicit removal of his language from the concrete functions which give it a point and alone justify its use. Functional analysis, on this view, has simply restored the language of the argument to its proper context.

Flew's case clearly depends on his analysis of the standard use of "freedom." For him the essential function of this word is to signify the absence of external constraint. That a choice may be fully determined by a person's glands or previous conditioning does not suffice to make us deny that the choice was "free."

It will not be denied that "free" and "freedom" are often and importantly employed in precisely this manner. To say that the parts of a machine are "moving freely" signifies not that their motions are uncaused or undetermined, but merely that there is no external constraint preventing them from acting in the way that they are fully (mechanically) determined to act. In the same way, we often talk of persons who have been in captivity "breaking free" or being "given their freedom." Here again "freedom" signifies the absence of iron bars, strait jackets and other external constraints; no covert suggestion about inner motives, glands, or the "springs of human action" is being made.

But, although this use of the word "freedom" is recognized and legitimate, it is not its only use; and Flew has been guilty of an oversight in supposing that his paradigm is adequate for the definition of *all* senses of "freedom" simply because it successfully represents *some* of them. In reference to choices, "freedom" in ordinary usage frequently entails "might-have-done-otherwise." Sociologists and psychologists and endocrinologists might meaningfully say about the criminal who broke from jail to "freedom" (in the first sense), that he was *not* "free" (in the second sense) to avoid killing the guard who tried to stop him: because of the guard's symbolic status as a father-figure (says the psychologist), because of the slum conditions in which he was reared to hate and fear all policemen (says the sociologist), because of overstimulation of his adrenal glands (says the physiologist). In such contexts to say that a man "was not free" is not to assert that he was handcuffed or at the point of a gun but to affirm that, given the caused causes in his make-up, no real alternative to his act was open to him.

Another, more relevant, context in which "freedom" is unconfusingly employed to signify the absence of constraint, external *or* internal, is moral discourse. The statement "Only free decisions deserve praise or blame" is properly taken not merely to exclude praise or blame from acts performed at bayonet point or not performed while externally constrained but also to deny the propriety of moral praise or blame directed at acts "wholly determined by caused causes" of an internal nature as well. "You ought to have rescued Mary," for example, makes no sense if Mary drowned in the Pacific while you were at the Atlantic Ocean. This falls under the head of "external" constraint. But blame for failure to rescue Mary is equally misdirected if (for caused causes) you do not know how to swim. Given your psychological and physiological make-up at that moment you were not *free* to swim to Mary's aid. You would have been "free" in the sense that no external constraint prevented you from plunging into the water; but your lack of knowledge "how to" held you a prisoner as surely as if you had been bound hand and foot on the beach. Here, in connection with moral praise and blame, everyone can understand the use of the word "free" to exclude all circumstances, external or internal, which makes "could-have-done-otherwise" an empty phrase.

I am not here even arguing that there are, in fact, "free acts" or "free choices" in the sense of the term which is important for moral judgment. This is a separate issue. What is vital to recognize is that without "freedom" (of the ethical paradigm) moral praise or blame cannot be bestowed upon *decisions*. One may still praise or blame *acts* on the basis of their consequences (if one is ready to grant hedonist or utilitarian or other criteria), but this for many ethical theorists including Kant will not be *moral* praise or blame. If an act happens to result in greater pleasure for the greatest number, though only by accident or by mistake or unconsciously, one may be grateful for its occurrence but he cannot give *moral* approbation to the agent. Similarly, if a tiger tears a lamb to shreds we may sorrow but we can hardly disapprove of the brute's morality.

Flew has failed to untangle several important threads in what is admittedly a knotty problem. He has analyzed "freedom" in terms of only one of its logically legitimate uses. He has likewise recognized only one sense of the words "good" and "evil." Actions which are the mere working out of necessity (mechanical, psychological) cannot be *morally* good or evil. God might, if omnipotent, have created a race which would be determined to act only in ways which we would call "good" on some criterion of goodness. But such a race would not be "free" in the sense which is important for morality; nor would all the "good" acts of Flew's ideal universe add up to a single moral decision.

But it is precisely *moral* evil which Flew is ostensibly discussing. His employment of a paradigm for "freedom" which brings out only the non-moral uses of this word has subtly shifted attention to something quite different. That which is no contradiction on Flew's (rather arbitrarily chosen) paradigm, which permits the logical compatibility of "free choice" and "complete causal determination," becomes a contradiction once again on the abandonment of this particular paradigm for a less ill-chosen one. And if the theist is talking about moral freedom, not mere freedom from external constraint, the free-will defense has not been "broken backed," as Flew hopes, but only lost sight of in this elaborate exercise in equivocation. Only by implicitly eliminating the possibility of all moral judgments can Flew assimilate *all* uses of "freedom" to the sort of "freedom" witnessed in the activity of an unobstructed sewing machine.

10

THE FAMILIAR FUNCTIONS OF THEOLOGICAL DISCOURSE

MOST OF THOSE who employ functional analysis to explore the nature of theological discourse seek more to understand the genuine use (or uses) of this language than to condemn its misuses. The tendency among these analysts is often to single out one or more familiar functions of language as the "real" logic of theological language.

Many philosophers are content with a relatively simple view. They recognize, as we have, the failure of theological discourse to compete with science as an "experimental, empirical" language. But at the same time they accept the premise of functional analysis, stated here by J. B. Coates, that "logic, if it is to have a useful bearing on life, must provide a justification for many of the ways in which men actually reason, seeing that that reason cannot be entirely fallacious as it serves them not too badly in numberless situations."[1]

The logic of theological speech can find its justification in doing a different job from that of the logic of science. As Coates puts it, "there are other positive uses of a belief in God which satisfy deeply felt needs to-day and do not seem to those who find benefit from them to express anything superstitious or unreasonable."[2] What are these "uses" for theistic belief? Coates suggests that the employment of religious phrases helps one to feel "more reassured about the world" by speaking of its relations to "another (better) world" and to feel more "at home" in this world by speaking of it as "created by a loving hand."

Coates, like many others, does not stop to inquire in what respects one is made to feel "at home" by using religious language, or to explore the source of the psychological power of theistic belief once its role as offering quasi-scientific "experimental" statements has been disallowed. More is needed; and much of the most creative work in contemporary philosophy of religion has been the effort to supply this "more."

I

Some philosophers, in spelling out more precisely the ways in which theological language functions, have emphasized what we may call (although they themselves frequently do not) "existential" uses. All men, despite their many differences, find themselves in a mode of existence such that they have certain fundamental features in common—man is in an "existential situation" which he did not choose but, rather, in Heidegger's metaphor, was "thrown" into.

A central fact about man's inescapable existential situation is that every individual is "one-who-must-die." Another is that each person is in the world as "one-who-is-finite." It is against the background of such features of man's existential situation, some philosophers point out, that his theological affirmations should be interpreted.

D. M. MacKinnon proposes that theological claims about an "afterlife" be examined more in terms of the existential discontent which gives rise to this language than in terms of any alleged descriptive content the word may have. As MacKinnon admits, the traditional arguments for life-after-death are logically "monstrous." "One cannot, if one is honest," he says, "ignore the extent to which metaphysical arguments, like those concerning immortality, have gained plausibility from a refusal to attend to the logic of our language."[3] Still, such arguments are important to the analyst. "For in them, surely, so much . . . is set out, albeit indirectly, of the inwardness of the person whose arguments they are."[4] Language about immortality stems from a deep discontent—a deep affirmation which comes from the whole man.

To put it very crudely, just what is it that is at stake for a person in this matter of immortality? What is it that is bothering him? Of course, you can show the queerness, the confusedness of the way in which the bother is expressing itself, when it does so by means of the traditional language of survival, and so on. You can discredit this means of expression by showing the logical confusions into which it plunges: but does that settle the perplexity, the issue in the mind of the bewildered person?[5]

What *is* the "bother" which MacKinnon alleges to be behind language of this sort? It is the fact that death, a clinical phenomenon, seems to have the last word—the last laugh—on human life. Our language about the afterlife has the real function, then, not of

. . . stretching or straining after inconceivable states of being. It has rather become a question of the way we regard the term of human life. Is it or is it not true that those who still mouth the logical vulgarities of traditional arguments concerning immortality do so because in the end they just cannot allow that the clinician has said or can say all that is to be significantly said about death?[6]

Theological talk about immortality and resurrection is not correctly to be understood as an illicit (and unsuccessful) "attempt to gain knowledge of fact without the discipline of experiment and reflective analysis." It is, we might say, the desperate (for some) or the confident (for others) affirmation by "one-who-must-die" that he *matters*.

Theological language not only allows man to affirm his significance in the face of death but also makes possible the confident acceptance of his existential situation as "one-who-is-finite." Philip Leon, like MacKinnon, refuses to reduce the logic of theological discourse to that of science. A basic difference distinguishes them: "Reflection upon this difference shows us that the unbeliever does not really contradict the believer, because they are simply using different languages. . . ."[7] Scientific statements derive their meaning from referring to things and events, but theological statements function entirely within the existing "theocentric life." One learns the real meaning of the latter "by an examination of their function, or their 'cash value,' or what they sum up, in that life."[8]

Sentences from the theological vocabulary like "God made the world" do not function, then, in the same way as "Wren made St. Paul's." On the contrary, such theological expressions, according to Leon, are

. . . not logical but existential, revelational, or inspirational; . . . they do not refer to God as a cause or agent; and . . . they do not connect

with him any particular item of reality except as an inseparable element
in the worshipper's life and as the focus of inspiration.[9]

Through them man, as "one-who-is-finite," contemplates the context of his existence in the world and, in "wonder or awe," accepts
it.

The analysis of theological language in terms of its "existential"
function undoubtedly reveals much concerning the logic of its use.
Even the language of the traditional theistic proofs has been sub-
jected to interpretation from this point of view, with interestingly
novel results: "God meets me in my present situation," E. L. Allen
declares, "and . . . all my arguments about Him have force only
as they admit of . . . an existential translation. . . ."[10]

But pointing out an "existential" use, where primary attention
is paid to "affirmative attitudes" or to vaguely specified "postures
taken towards existence," does not seem to account for other less
rarefied functions of theological discourse. Most philosophers of language, rightly or wrongly, suspect the presence of a good deal of
woolliness in "existential" talk wherever found—a woolliness which
can be avoided only by more careful attention to specifics.

II

R. B. Braithwaite and others are quite prepared to be specific
about how theological language functions. If, as functional analysis
recognizes, "the meaning of any statement . . . will be taken as
being given by the way it is used,"[11] then the analysis of theological
statements must rest on a basis of "empirical enquiry" since, Braithwaite says, "a statement need not itself be empirically verifiable,
but that it is used in a particular way is always a straightforwardly
empirical proposition."[12] The results of such an inquiry, he tells us,
show that "the primary element in this use is that the religious
assertion is used as a moral assertion."[13]

Those who accept this analysis of theological language, emphasizing the "ethical" function of theological speech, are not intent—as
are the verificational analysts—on reducing ethical discourse to the
mere expressing of emotional approval or disapproval. Braithwaite
agrees that this "emotivist" theory of ethical language does account
for its empirical unverifiability; but, he says, the most important
aspect of moral utterances is ignored on the verificationist's approach: ethical statements function as the expression of an *intention*

to act in certain ways under certain circumstances. Moral discourse is conative rather than purely emotive; when one makes an ethical assertion one is in fact "subscribing to a policy of action," one is engaging in an act of "self-commitment" to a general pattern of behavior. The theist might well object, Braithwaite sees, to an analysis of his language which equates it with ethical language treated as merely emotive.

This objection, however, does not seem to me to apply to treating religious assertions in the conative way in which recent moral philosophers have treated moral statements—as being primarily declarations of adherence to a policy of action, declarations of commitment to a way of life.[14]

Quite the contrary, this analysis of theological assertions directly supports the theist's constant insistence that Christian doctrine must spring from and encourage the life of the Christian community.

What is the essential function of Christian discourse, then, if its meaning is essentially that of ethical language dedicating the user to a certain course of action? This is a complex question, but Braithwaite suggests that the typical meaning of the language of Christianity is found in "claiming intentions to follow an agapeistic way of life. . . ."[15] An "agapeistic" ethic is one which demands not only overt actions of *agape* (other-centered charity) modeled after the life of Christ but also—more difficult yet—the commitment of the very feelings and emotional attitudes of the Christian.

Because of this dual demand on one who has committed himself to an agapeistic ethic by sincerely using Christian phrases, the language of theistic doctrine must involve a second, ethically *supporting,* function. It is in the form of particular "stories," the function of which is to give psychological strength in times of weakness or temptation and to evoke the proper ethical attitudes. The stories peculiar to the different religions distinguish the various faiths from one another even where there is no difference in ethical commitment; but the story-language alone is not fully religious language (this would be indistinguishable from the mythical or fictional or historical uses of language), since reading about (and appreciating) the Buddha does not inevitably make one a Buddhist, and reading about the Christ is a different thing from being a Christian. Only the combination of psychologically effective stories (whether or not they are believed as "literally true" makes no difference, Braith-waite holds, as long as their causal power is unimpaired) with a commitment of the self to a policy of life associated with these stories constitutes genuinely theological language.

In making this analysis of the use of theological language Braith-waite has offered another justification for it, because ethical systems —vitally important to the quality of our social existence—are no-toriously difficult to follow in practice. If religious language has been found to have an important role to play in the support of ethical programs both by encouraging men to make common com-mitments to a way of life and by strengthening them in the carry-ing out of these commitments, then it is a most important and most legitimate sort of speech. Braithwaite's analysis, he hopes, has also revealed the importance of our employing the *right* religious lan-guage, in as much as great practical consequences spring from one's choice of ethical commitment. Ultimately, of course, personal de-cision must determine the sort of commitment, and thus the kind of language, which we employ; but in preparing to make that de-cision the relevance of rational and empirical discussion is far greater than we might expect. Our religion will reflect our practical aims and our social aspirations; religious language is intimately connected to our commitment to conduct, and therefore, "in con-sidering what conduct to intend to practise, it is highly relevant whether or not the consequences of practising that conduct are such as one would intend to secure."[16]

E. L. Mascall says of Braithwaite's analysis in his polemical little book *Words and Images* that it is "surely very much less than the truth." He objects in particular to Braithwaite's supposition that Christianity could be content with his conative view of theological language. The essentials of Christian belief are not rigidly defined, Mascall admits, but "it is surely undeniable that Christianity de-mands personal commitment not to a personal way of life (what-ever that extremely vague phrase may mean), but to the concrete historical person Jesus of Nazareth."[17]

This, however, is just what Braithwaite's avowed principles will not allow him to say, whatever may be the implications of his religious prac-tices. For to say this would be to imply that some at least of the Gospel stories were factually true, and indeed that the person of whom they tell is still alive and can be met with today.[18]

It is possible to agree with Mascall that traditional Christianity is incompatible with Braithwaite's interpretation of the function of theological language if this interpretation is taken as exhaustive and complete, and still to feel that Mascall's criticism is beside the point. In the first place it is not easy to see how commitment to a "concrete historical person" necessarily "implies" that this person is "still alive" or that he "can be met with today." No doubt commitment to a concrete historical person (whatever *that* extremely vague phrase may mean) does entail belief that such a person existed. *Some* "stories" about the person would need to be considered true. But the stories which attributed supernatural powers or status to this concrete person might not be among the group of stories so considered. Among liberal Christians they often have not been. One's commitment might be to a concrete person now held in reverent memory. Second, what, specifically, is meant by "commitment to Jesus Christ as a concrete historical person"? Is not the understanding of the phrase intimately bound up with subscription to an agapeistic way of life? Can Mascall explicate its meaning without relying on what Braithwaite would call a conative theory and without mentioning *"agape"?* Was it not Christ himself who is reported to have said (in one of the "stories" of Christianity), "Ye are my disciples if ye do the things I command . . ."? Finally, the analysis of theological speech in terms of "ethical" functions is not to be judged, as Mascall seems to suppose, solely on the basis of its compatibility with traditional Christian theism; the interpretation of the significance of Christian theism awaits an adequate analysis of theological discourse.

Christianity as normally understood, however, is not explicated without distortion by Braithwaite's techniques. Mascall is on firm ground here. Ronald Hepburn, too, finds Braithwaite guilty of attempting to gloss over the difference between traditional Christian faith and the findings of modern philosophy. Hepburn, whose own views are in some respects a refinement of Braithwaite's position, recognizes the incompatibility of his philosophical conclusions with traditional Christian belief—and boldly rejects Christianity.

What is validly religious about Christianity, however, is well expressed, he believes, by reference to the "fortifying of morality by parable." But at two points Hepburn goes beyond Braithwaite in defining more specifically what kind of ethical commitment is characteristically "religious." Like Braithwaite, Hepburn contends that

. . . the believer commits himself to a pattern of ethical behaviour. This way of life is simply decided for as an ultimate moral choice: empirical facts will be relevant to his choice, but he can *derive* his decision from no facts whatever, not even from commands of God, should he believe in a God.[19]

But whereas Braithwaite is content to refer vaguely to "stories" as supporting this commitment, Hepburn requires the "stories" (or "parables," as he calls them) both to be "tightly cohering" and to be of a type "that vividly expresses the way of life chosen" while it psychologically "inspires the believer to implement it in practice." Beyond this, and perhaps most important of all, Hepburn insists that the "parable" must not be partial or trivial. "The parable and its associated pattern of behaviour legislate not for any *fraction* of the believer's life, but for every aspect of it. It commands his supreme loyalty and determines his total imaginative vision of nature and man."[20]

Hepburn defends his view that these criteria are sufficient for defining religion by showing that he has in no way eliminated the possibility of fellowship in shared parables, that he is not committed to a life of immorality or to a view of the universe as "hostile" just because he has rejected the Christian faith, that his understanding of religion permits growth and a sense of spiritual "pilgrimage," that his possible range of inspiring parables is far richer than that offered by any particular historic religion, and that "in so far as a story or parable delineates a way of life that we judge to be valuable, it is not of paramount importance whether or not the story or parable is historically true. It can do its job equally well if fictitious; sometimes better."[21]

Hepburn's final point, fundamental to all theories which would find an adequate interpretation of theological discourse in its "ethical" function, must seriously be questioned. A. C. Ewing, for example, points out that both emotivist and conativist interpretations of theism sacrifice the element which alone gives power to an emotion or justifies a policy of action—the element of *belief*. "Emotion . . . requires some objective belief, true or false, about the real to support it for long. . . ."[22] In so far as fictitious stories are influential it is because they succeed in pointing up "factors present in real life." The "stories" of religion deal with those things which a person considers to be most important, and "it is difficult to see how they could long survive the thorough conviction that these . . . could not possibly be true."[23] C. H. Whitely, again, offers an example to illustrate the importance of belief, whether or not belief happens to be true.

Let us suppose, what must sometimes be the case, that the whole benefit a neurotic derives from his visit to a psychiatrist arises from the fact that on the psychiatrist's couch, and nowhere else, he is able to relax and unburden his mind of its anxieties. Then it would be true that he would be equally benefited if the psychiatrist was an ignoramus, or was not listening, or even was not there at all. But it would not be true that he would be equally, or at all, benefited if he *believed* that the psychiatrist was an ignoramus, or not listening, or not there.[24]

R. M. Hare, in a chapter entitled "Religion and Morals" (one of the ablest recent analyses of the intertwined languages of ethics and theology), agrees that while theological speech has an important moral component the ethical function is not the *distinctive* function of theological statements. "The moral judgments, as we may say, arise out of the religious belief; they do not constitute it."[25] What is distinctive about theological assertions is the belief-content, then; or, to be more precise, it is to be found in *what* is believed. This content of belief is distinctive, to Hare, because although it is similar to ordinary factual belief in some respects, it is radically different from such factual belief in others. Let us turn from the popular but incomplete analysis of theological language in its ethical function, then, to Hare's view of theological discourse as having a use that is primarily "quasi-factual."

III

Theological statements appear at one level of analysis to be used in the straightforward assertion of fact. The sentence "Jesus is the Son of God" has what looks like the status of factual belief in Christian practice. Just as one often changes his views as to how he ought to behave in certain circumstances in the light of changed beliefs about the facts of the case, so (Hare points out)

St. Paul thought that he ought to stop persecuting Christians because he had changed his belief about a specifically religious matter which was not itself a matter of how one ought to behave, but more like a matter of fact; he had come to believe that Jesus was the Christ, the Son of God.[26]

This "factual" statement, however, is not stating what we normally consider a fact at all. It is not merely equivalent to all the factual assertions which could be made truthfully about Jesus of Nazareth. Many of the disciples' contemporaries knew all the *facts* about Jesus—his teachings, his healings, and so on—but refused to declare, with St. Peter, "Thou art the Christ!" For those who chose to adopt them, alternative interpretations of all the facts about Jesus were available. Did he claim a special relationship to God? He was an impostor and a liar. Did he perform miracles? He was an agent of Beelzebub. When two persons can agree on all the facts and still differ on whether they should say "Jesus is the Christ, the Son of God," then their disagreement is not a factual one; it is a conflict in attitudes, and attitudes, of course, are intimately bound up with "policies of action."

Here is the uniqueness of theological discourse, then, which marks it off from ethical language on the one hand and factual-scientific language on the other. "If we take religious language as a whole, it is too factual to be called specifically moral, and yet too closely bound up with our conduct to be called in the ordinary sense factual."[27] But the "quasi-factual" function of theological statements differs even from all other evaluative discourse (for example, the language of aesthetics) by virtue of the *kind* of attitude which theism springs from and engenders. Here Hepburn's insight is retained that religion has essentially to do with what is overwhelmingly important to one—one's "ultimate concern," in Paul Tillich's phrase—and Hare puts it:

. . . the *facts* that religious discourse deals with are perfectly ordinary empirical facts like what happens when you pray; but we are tempted to call them supernatural facts because our whole way of living is organized round them; they have for us value, relevance, importance, which they would not have if we were atheists.[28]

Still, Hare warns, *no* facts, however "ordinary," can be known apart from the active discriminating power of our minds or independent of our dispositions to accept criteria for distinguishing "facts" from "illusions." Some attitude, like religious attitudes, *must* be logically prior to any facts, since "there is no distinction between fact and illusion for a person who does not take up a certain attitude to the world."[29] Now we understand more fully Hare's concept, mentioned earlier, of a *blik;* and we see its relevance to a fuller analysis of the possibility of knowledge. All knowledge depends on attitudes and dispositions which transcend the particular "facts" made possible by them. "The facts" cannot disprove such ultimate categories of thought, because what we are willing to recognize as a "fact" is relative to the ultimate category, or *blik.* If religious quasi-factual statements have a large attitudinal component, they are at least not in bad company nor do they function less importantly than "ordinary factual" statements. Hare concludes "very tentatively":

> Now Christians believe that God created the world out of chaos, or out of nothing, in the sense of no *thing.* . . . Is it possible that this is our way of expressing the truth that without belief in a divine order—a belief expressed in other terms by means of worshipping assent to principles for discriminating between fact and illusion—there could be no belief in matters of fact or in real objects? Certainly it is salutary to recognize that *even* our belief in so-called hard facts rests in the end on a faith, a commitment, which is not in or to facts, but in that without which there would not be any facts.[30]

It seems most unlikely that many theists will agree with Hare that their statements about a "divine order" are equivalent to statements made in a worshipful attitude about the epistemological importance of *bliks,* but all will be grateful for his penetrating analysis of the ways in which theological statements are like—and unlike—factual assertions, for his timely reaffirmation of the important role of belief-plus-attitude in theological language, and for his insistence on the fundamental importance of religious attitude-beliefs for life and knowledge.

IV

Hare shows that Christians and non-Christians are not, strictly speaking, disputing over *facts* when they argue over the nature of Christ. But Professor John Wisdom, who agrees that no "facts" in the sense of *predictions* are at issue between the theist and the atheist, points out a more subtle way in which "the facts" may figure in theological dispute. In Wisdom's analysis, theological discourse has an "attention-directing" function which is too frequently overlooked by those who suppose that "the facts" are entirely "given."

Fundamental for Wisdom is the recognition that "it is possible to have before one's eyes all the items of a pattern and still to miss the pattern."[31] Just as important as having all the facts before one and having some attitude toward these facts (two aspects distinguished by Hare) is noticing the patterns composed by the facts. As Wisdom notes:

"A difference as to the facts," "a discovery," "a revelation," these phrases cover many things. Discoveries have been made not only by Christopher Columbus and Pasteur, but also by Tolstoy and Dostoievsky and Freud. Things are revealed to us not only by the scientists with microscopes, but also by the poets, the prophets, and the painters. What is so isn't merely a matter of "the facts."[32]

It is in this connection that Wisdom offers his famous parable of the two gardeners (made use of by Antony Flew, as we noticed earlier, with the technique of verificational analysis). Wisdom, at the start, uses his parable to illustrate the unfalsifiable (and therefore non-experimental) nature of a belief in "an absolutely undetectable gardener." When all the facts and probable facts are entirely agreed upon, one man continues to say, "There is no gardener," while the other insists, "There is a gardener, though he is manifested only in the facts upon which we agree"; then "with this difference in what they say about the gardener goes a difference in how they feel towards the garden, in spite of the fact that neither expects anything of it which the other does not expect."[33]

But while Flew is content to rest his case against theological discourse (so similar to the language about the garden) on the discovery of its unfalsifiable character, Wisdom uses his parable as a starting-point from which to learn what, if it is not experimental, the logic of theological discourse can be. Perhaps a great deal of the difference between theists and atheists can be put down to a matter of mere feelings, he says, but it is sheer distortion to suppose that *all* difference is attitudinal and non-cognitive (and therefore "stating nothing"). On the contrary,

, . . the disputants speak as if they are concerned with a matter of scientific fact, or of trans-sensual, trans-scientific and metaphysical fact, but still of fact and still a matter about which reasons for and against may be offered, although no scientific reasons in the sense of field surveys for fossils or experiments on delinquents are to the point.[34]

The function of theological discourse, Wisdom concludes, is to *direct our attention* to patterns in "the facts." Just because we recognize that theological claims are not open to the logic of experimental science,

> . . . *we must not forthwith assume that there is no right and wrong about it,* no rationality or irrationality, no appropriateness or inappropriateness, no procedure which tends to settle it, *nor even that this procedure is in no sense a discovery of new facts.*[35]

As Wisdom puts it in terms of his parable,

> Our two gardeners even when they had reached the stage when neither expected any experimental result which the other did not, might yet have continued the dispute, each presenting and re-presenting the features of the garden favouring his hypothesis, that is, fitting his model for describing the accepted fact; each emphasizing the pattern he wishes to emphasize.[36]

In like manner, techniques for arguing meaningfully about theological issues are techniques of pointing up features in the facts which may not have been noticed, taking attention away from features which obscure the pattern one finds. Here the language we employ, including our choice of similes and metaphors, our stock of concepts generally, is of the essence. An apt choice of language may direct attention to a pattern which had been "seen" but not "noticed"; misuse of language may blur and distort and prevent the pattern from being noticed. "The question 'What's in a name?' is engaging," Wisdom says, "because we are inclined to answer both 'Nothing' and 'Very much.' " And as we can now see, "this 'Very much' has more than one source."[37]

It may be that no practical difference will result from using one kind of language rather than another, but, as Wisdom has pointed out, there are other kinds of important differences than practical ones. "New knowledge made it necessary either to give up saying 'The sun is sinking' or to give the words a new meaning." In some cases old locutions offer more depth of insight than modern paraphrases. Psychology in our day has revealed new depths of personality, new "facts," which were not suspected by any but the religious.

Such discoveries remind us forcefully of the stress which theism has traditionally placed on the "Kingdom within." May there not be good reason to continue to use the concepts of religion which direct our attention to facts that might otherwise go unnoticed? May we not honor the language of Elijah, who "found that God was not in the wind, nor in the thunder, but in a still small voice"?

In these ways, therefore, Wisdom would urge that the language of theology is related to "the facts." No strict experimental relation is tenable, but this does not reduce the status of theological speech to "merely emotive" burblings. Attitudes play an important role but do not function as the whole motivating force behind religious statements. The functions of theological discourse are complex.

> And though we shall need to emphasize how much "There is a God" evinces an attitude to the familiar we shall find in the end that it also evinces some recognition of patterns in time easily missed and that, therefore, difference as to there being any gods is in part a difference as to what is so and therefore as to the facts, though not in the simple ways which first occurred to us.[38]

The accounts of the uses of theological discourse which we have examined in this chapter have increased in complexity. From the simple suggestion that the function of theological speech is to "reassure," through the more highly developed "existential," "ethical," and "quasi-factual" views to the subtle interweaving of several functions in the "attention-directing" interpretation, the sincere attempt has been made to appreciate realistically the essential use or uses of theological language.

But despite differences, the foregoing analyses have been alike in one major respect: they have all sought to understand the logic of theological discourse exhaustively in terms of functions which language may serve outside the strictly theological context. Many non-religious uses of language may "reassure" one or make one feel "at home" in the world. What, we still want to know, is the distinguishing characteristic of the kind of "reassurance" derived from singing "This is my Father's world"? Existential affirmations, again, need not be theistic in character. What is the difference between affirming one's situation in existence by means of theological language, with Marcel, and by means of self-consciously atheistic language, with Sartre? Ethical language, as we have seen, is intimately related but not identical to theological language—even with the addition of "stories" taken as psychological strengthening-medicine. The "quasi-factual" function of language is discovered to be none other than the non-descriptive evaluative function of the language of morals and aesthetics raised to a new pitch of importance. And language is used in its "attention-directing" role, Wisdom insists, not merely in theological but also in aesthetic and other discussions. What is distinctive about theological language is briefly treated, if at all.

It may, of course, be true that there is in fact nothing distinctive about the logic of theological discourse, that it is a special form of another kind of language like that of ethics or aesthetics—or a combination of several of these languages. Many would claim that the best possible justification for theological language would be to show this to be the case. But other contemporary philosophical voices have been raised to insist that there is more which is distinctive to theological discourse than the unaccountable appearance within it of the three-letter word "God." Otherwise, they point out, it would be difficult to see why theists themselves claim that there is a fundamental difference between their assertions and the words of poetry or the exhortations of ethics.

11

THE UNIQUE FUNCTIONS OF
THEOLOGICAL DISCOURSE

THOSE WHO ARE unconvinced by the attempts to show theological discourse to be somehow a misuse of language, and yet who are unready to allow theism to be interpreted exhaustively in terms other than distinctively theistic, must bear the burden of showing that theological language has a unique use in addition to (or instead of) the functions which we examined in the last chapter. Various suggested candidates for this unique function demand our attention.

I

A popular method intended to isolate the unique logic of theological discourse has been to speak of the "worshipful" function of theological speech. We have already seen the beginnings of such an analysis in R. M. Hare's discussion of the "quasi-factual" function of theological statements where he distinguishes the type of attitude characteristic of religion as "worshiping" assent.

J. J. C. Smart and E. L. Allen have advanced this analysis further by claiming to show that the essential use given to theological language—even apparently discursive language like the language of theistic proofs—is really "worshipful." Allen suggests that the secret of the vitality of the often refuted ontological argument is its employment in a "worshipful" act where the mind is flooded with religious apprehension.[1] Smart offers a similar treatment of the cosmological and teleological arguments. The cosmological argument reflects the "necessity" of God, but not a "necessity" of the kind traditionally supposed, because "it is not a logical necessity that God exists. But it would clearly upset the structure of our *religious attitudes* in the most violent way if we denied it or even entertained the possibility of its falsehood."[2] Similarly, the teleological argument is relevant to religious attitudes of worship, according to Smart. It points to facts about the grandeur and majesty of the universe which have a "powerful effect" on the mind capable of feeling "the religious type of awe." "That is, the argument from design is in reality no argument . . . but it is a potent instrument in heightening religious emotions."[3]

It will be apparent, however, that as an attempt at isolating some uniquely religious factor inherent in theological discourse the approach is of little help. Our understanding is hardly advanced by being told that "religious" apprehension, "religious" emotions, or "religious" awe is at stake. We should previously need to understand what is characteristic of religion if such labels are to be useful to us. Before we are benefited by being told that theological statements serve a "worshipful" function, we must understand what it is to worship.

Hare, it may be recalled, attempts to explain the nature of worship in terms of personal evaluations of supreme importance, reminding us, perhaps unintentionally, of Paul Tillich's definition of religion as "ultimate concern." Hare recognizes, however, that some evaluations of supreme importance may be directed toward objects which, nevertheless, are not "worthy objects of worship." He hopes to clarify his position by specifying that "worship" is offered only to realities considered to be "personal," but ends (as he himself suspects) by setting up the tautology "if object of worship, then 'personal' "—explaining neither the logic of his new key term, "personal," nor the manner in which such "worshipful" evaluations are manifested if they ever occur.

II

Willem Zuurdeeg attempts to supply a full description of the uniquely theological logic that is only named by calling it "religious" or "worshipful." The gist of his elaborate treatment of this question in *An Analytical Philosophy of Religion* is that theological language is not "indicative" (referring to the empirical world) nor "analytical" (relating definitions to one another) but "convictional." Convictional language, says Zuurdeeg, refers to "reality"; but it is not possible or desirable to raise the question of whether or not this reference is veridical.

Both convictional and indicative languages refer to "reality." Here lies a crucial problem. The assertion that both languages refer to "reality" does not imply any judgment on the part of the analytical philosopher about the nature of these "realities," for example, as to whether or not they are illusionary. It is not the analytical philosopher's business to decide whether the reality meant in a certain language is "really" there or not. The only thing he can do is to notice that if human beings speak either indicative or convictional language they refer to something which is "real" *for them.*[4]

Convictional language, furthermore, refers to "all the reality there is," not just to some aspect of reality as does the indicative language of the sciences. Consequently, convictional language has far deeper roots in the personalities of its employers than less totalitarian forms of discourse. More accurately, convictional language *is* the person who speaks. "Man-who-speaks," *homo loquens,* does not merely use convictional language as he would use—and discard —a tool; he is totally involved in his convictions and therefore *is* his convictions. Religious language, what I have called the language of living faith, is such convictional language, for Zuurdeeg; the language of systematic theology, on the other hand, is convictional language *employed* (not merely "used") to give an account of life which "makes sense."

Thus equipped, Zuurdeeg feels able to distinguish the precise place of religious and systematic forms of theological speech. Religious language and moral language are both convictional languages, but religious language differs from moral language by referring "in the first place to the meaning of the All"[5] rather than primarily to evaluations of human behavior. The difference between the language of systematic theology and metaphysical discourse (both "employ-languages") lies in the fact that systematic language, like the language of living faith and ethics, does not deny that it is a convictional language, "whereas metaphysical language presupposes the claim that it possesses a purely rational basis."[6]

The testing of this discourse which, according to Zuurdeeg, somehow "makes sense" is not an easy matter. Since "we *are* our convictions," an attack on our convictional language will be resisted as an attack on ourselves. Logic is beside the point. "There are neither scientific nor philosophical proofs or arguments which can validate or invalidate any conviction."[7] "Consequently, it seems necessary to drop the term 'logical analysis' for the philosophical activity which deals with convictional language."[8]

Zuurdeeg's analysis suffers from a blithe disregard for the "really real" beyond the "situation" of man-who-speaks. Strict application of his view would lead to the acknowledgment of an incredible welter of convictional "realities" to which the check even of logical consistency would be inappropriate. But, despite its shortcomings, it succeeds in emphasizing the radical difference between language which is "merely used," that is, speech from which the speaker is entirely distinct, and language which is intimately bound up with the speaker's most fundamental appraisal of himself. Whatever the innermost logic of theological discourse, it is not language which is taken lightly. Somehow persons who use it feel they have a stake in it of a more serious kind than is possible in non-theological languages. To paraphrase Gabriel Marcel, the issues discussed in theological speech "encroach on their own utterers."

III

In contrast to Zuurdeeg's "non-logical" understanding of theological discourse as "convictional," related analyses in terms of its function in "commitment" may be offered on the basis of close attention to logic.

I. T. Ramsey, who is criticized by Zuurdeeg for his interest in the "cold artificialities" of logic in connection with theological speech, seeks to establish the unique character of theological discourse on the logical "oddness" of the theist's language and on the functions which this "oddness" serves in "evoking the distinctly theological situation" (i.e., experience) and expressing the resulting commitment. It is characteristic of the "theological situation" that one suddenly apprehends the personal where others (and perhaps oneself, at a different moment) find only the impersonal. A word drawn from an alien context, another "universe of discourse," Ramsey says, may by its very logical impropriety cause the "ice to break," the "penny to drop," reveal a new *Gestalt* of "I-thou" personal confrontation where only "I-it" impersonality was present a moment before.

Religious "situations" deal with one's sudden "discernment" of personal "depth" within the whole universe. And "with this discernment there now goes a personal commitment" to what "will not be exhaustively unpacked in scientific language, however far those languages go."[9] Ramsey finds this analysis applicable even to language ostensibly employed in discursive argument. It, too, is aiming at "personal revolution" away from a vision of the world which is "flat" or lacking in "depth."

So we see religious commitment as a *total* commitment to the *whole* universe; something in relation to which argument has only a very odd function; its purpose being to tell such a tale as evokes the "insight," the "discernment" from which the commitment follows as a response.[10]

Ramsey distinguishes three ways in which theological language functions to evoke the religious "situation" and occasion the religious commitment. First, the formal structure of theological speech is designed to negate and negate and negate, until "the penny drops" and the experience and commitment-response are elicited. Second, theological statements may attempt to bring about the final commitment by approaching asymptotically such limiting (and unthinkable) concepts as divine "unity," "simplicity," or "perfection," until "the ice breaks" for the listener. Third, the religious "situation" is brought about by theological language through its application of logically inappropriate "qualifiers" to straightforward "models" drawn from ordinary speech: that is, to the model-words "wise," "good," "cause," and so on, are attached (respectively) the odd qualifiers "infinitely," "perfectly," "first," and the like. Admittedly these qualifiers distort and negate the ordinary meaning of the models with which they are associated, but their function is not to give their models a certain kind of empirical relevance but to "develop a model in a certain direction" in order to make the religious situation "come alive."

Ramsey is extremely sensitive to the accusation that he has reduced the theological situation to a kind of subjectivism. His main defense against this charge is stated as follows:

There is no question of a characteristically religious situation being merely "emotional," if that word is thought to claim that the characteristic features we have been mentioning are entirely (in some sense or other) "subjective." Let us emphasize, without any possibility of misunderstanding, that all these situations, . . . when they occur, have an *objective* reference and are, as all situations, *subject-object* in structure. When situations "come alive," or the "ice breaks," there is objective "depth" in these situations along with and alongside any subjective changes.[11]

Although Ramsey has here succeeded in "emphasizing" his view, he has not advanced a step toward defending it. He fails to deal with illusions or the place of hallucination in experience. These, too, would no doubt be "subject-object" in structure; but would Ramsey be content to have "characteristically religious situations" considered in this light? He is quite correct in asserting that religious experience has a high degree of "intentionality," as we have recognized earlier, but is he not confusing "experiencing-*as*-objective" with having experience *of* the objective?

Ramsey is by no means alone when he emphasizes the function of theological statements in personal commitment. Alasdair MacIntyre finds the logic of theological speech to be essentially one of self-commitment to an authority; but for him the commitment is not properly regarded as to "the whole universe." As we saw earlier, MacIntyre is convinced that theism does not rest upon firm epistemological foundations. There can be no philosophical justification for theological language, he concludes; and it is not essential that such a justification can be found. "The philosopher is not concerned *qua* philosopher to offer an account of religion that will make religion appear logically reputable, but only to describe how religious language is in fact used."[12] This philosophical account will prove, as has been done already, that theological statements are not hypotheses; or, as MacIntyre puts it, "at least if they are they are very bad ones." At the same time, an accurate description of theological discourse will show, as we have noticed, that many theological statements claim that "God" is a being who works in history, that "God has done this and not that, is like this and not that." The theist here speaks in myths. He tells stories about the "mighty acts of God," and about the way that "God has acted" in his own life. But to say this is not enough, MacIntyre insists, for up to this point nothing has been said which would be incompatible with the "ethical-function" theories of Braithwaite or Hepburn. The crucial step for the theist, says MacIntyre, is commitment to *belief* in these myths as more than useful or inspiring stories. In the distinctively theological use of his language, "the religious believer commits himself in his use of myth to the view that these stories are in some way or other stories about a real being, God, acting in the world that we are acquainted with in ordinary experience."[13]

What for MacIntyre distinguishes the theological from other uses of language, then, is commitment to belief in stories about God; and what distinguishes one religion from another, within the theological context, are the authoritative criteria implicitly accepted by this self-commitment. Every religion, every particular religious language within the general class of theological discourse, possesses its own ultimate criteria. "Every religion," indeed, "is defined by reference to what it accepts as an authoritative criterion in religious matters."[14] It is by this ultimate criterion that any religious belief must finally be justified. "We justify a particular religious belief by showing its place in the total religious conception; we justify a religious belief as a whole by referring to authority."[15] And the very meaning of "ultimate criterion" or "authority" indicates that no "justification" is possible—by definition, if "ultimate" is taken seriously—for the criterion itself. "Religion is justified only by referring to a religious acceptance of authority. And this means, if you like, that religion as a whole lacks any justification."[16]

Sheer commitment to the authority of some ultimate criterion for theological statements may, in fact, be characteristic of some groups of theists, notably Muslims and Christian followers of the logic of obedience, but the critical reader is forced to wonder whether MacIntyre's account of the logic of theological discourse fulfills his own philosophical ideal of an accurate description of the bulk of theistic discussion. The history of apologetics—which is inseparable from the history of theistic thought as a whole—is a standing refutation of MacIntyre's refusal to admit that theological language can have a use in attempting to justify itself before objective criteria of reason and evidence. MacIntyre is convinced that no *valid* use of this kind is possible; many modern theologians as well as philosophers would agree. But if MacIntyre moves from this conviction to the conclusion that the "real" use of theological statements cannot be apologetic but must be understood only as utterance of—and challenge to—commitment, then he is cutting the coat of theological language to fit the cloth provided by his understanding of philosophical analysis. He is failing in his self-defined philosophical job of describing and is subtly at work providing a justification of sorts for this language—though not a "logical" justification, to be sure, since commitment to ultimate criteria must transcend the criteria of logic (even if logic itself is the object of one's commitment).

I am convinced, as will be evident in the next chapter, that theological discourse is misunderstood if it is interpreted, as in MacIntyre's view, as nothing but an exercise in the arbitrary. But though theological speech is not entirely a matter of mere acceptance of authority, neither is it to be understood apart from personal faith-commitment. By turning our attention to this aspect of the functioning of theological discourse, MacIntyre has advanced our understanding. There are discernible points where theism must "convert," as MacIntyre tells us; but it must attempt conversion not *instead of* argument so much as for the *sake of* meaningful argument concerning "ultimate questions" of human life.

IV

The thoughtful discussion provided by Ian Crombie in *Faith and Logic* combines many of the points of view which have been examined in this chapter.

Crombie deals with the formal anomalies present in theological discourse, as does Ian Ramsey. Unlike Ramsey, Crombie attends less to the psychological effects of these logical peculiarities than to the semantic properties of referring and describing which they make possible. The logical "oddness" of theological speech, according to Crombie, fixes the "reference range" of theological discourse (that is, roughly specifies the general limits of what is being talked about) by eliminating all improper objects of reference (like finite things or empirical events) from theistic discussion and by suggesting the realms of non-theological discourse (ethical, historical, cosmological, and so on) to which theological speech is somehow relevant. Within this general "reference range," a concept of the divine is specified by reference to a being characterized by *absence* of the human limitations of finitude, space-time location, and the like—which limitations we can easily *feel* as dissatisfactions even while we are unable to *conceive* positively the kind of being which would be free from such dissatisfactions. Our "concept of God" is no concept in the sense of an idea, then; but Crombie insists that if we follow his directions for narrowing the reference of the word "God," "it is extravagant to say that we have no notion whatsoever of how the word is used."[17]

Once given the reference of theological discourse, theological talk in parables gains a new dimension of significance. The words of a theological parable retain their ordinary meanings, Crombie insists (in a point of agreement with MacIntyre), and it is only within the parable that we understand what words mean in their theological application: in the story of the Prodigal Son, for example, we come to understand the "love" of God univocally with reference to the kind of "love" a charitable human father might exhibit in running to forgive his penitent son. All language about God is thus parabolical. But it is more than *mere* parable, because the parables are referred to our concept of God beyond the parable, and referred, in faith, as true to the reality which we cannot positively comprehend.

The point of a parable is that you do not suppose that there is any literal resemblance between the truth which is expressed and the story which expresses it, but you do suppose that if you accept the story, not as a true literal account, but as a faithful parable, you will not be misled as to the nature of the underlying reality.[18]

Why, someone asks, should *these* parables be referred to God rather than others? To this question Crombie replies basically in terms of personal commitment. Christians simply find themselves "impelled" to accept Christ as divine and therefore authoritative for the reference of their parabolical theological statements. Christ is the supreme image of God; language about God has its ultimate justification in commitment to the Christ-image as faithful. But Crombie, unlike MacIntyre, does not rest the entire justification of theological parables on sheer acceptance of Christian authorities: he hints, also, that independent justification—at least to a limited degree—is possible. To speak of God in terms of Christian images, like that of "creator of the world," is controversial, Crombie admits, but the choice of these images over others is not arbitrary.

Our use of this image . . . is based on two things: firstly on the fact that we find ourselves impelled to regard the events recorded in the Bible and found in the life of the Church as the communication of a transcendent being, and that the image is an essential part of this com-

munication; secondly on the fact that the more we try to understand
the world in the light of this image, the better our understanding of the
world becomes.[19]

It is Crombie's second point which distinguishes his position from
MacIntyre's logic of sheer commitment. If one is merely "impelled"
to regard the Bible and the Church as authoritative, little discussion
will be fruitful with one who is not so "impelled," but if one's theological images are capable of *illuminating one's understanding of
the world,* then argument will be not only possible but also, perhaps,
of considerable importance to others besides oneself. Crombie does
not develop this hint, though he places "illumination" on a par
with "impulsion" as fundamental to the justification of theological
language. "These two things conspiring together," he concludes,
"are our authority for the use of the image, and for our affirming
it."[20]

Since Crombie does not explore the implications of his suggestion,
it may be profitable for us to do so in the following chapter, where,
I hope, the threads of our discussion may be drawn together.

12

THE MANIFOLD LOGIC
OF THEISM

WE HAVE EXAMINED many points of view in the course of the preceding chapters, and although I have tried to show that various approaches to theological language fall into discernible patterns, a number of questions have been raised in the course of the discussion which need more careful attention. While these profound problems cannot begin to be treated adequately in the limited space remaining, or within the modest purposes of this book, it may further clarify the issues with which we have been dealing if I can place the controversy over theological discourse within a wider understanding of linguistic signification. Perhaps only in this way will we be able to appreciate fully the manifold nature of the logic of theism.

I

Three factors are present in every "signification-situation" (as we shall call the situation wherein language purports to signify a "fact" of some kind, a state of affairs, or "something that is the case") : first, there is the factor of the language itself, the presence of marks or sounds which serve to signify; second, there is the factor of the language-using agent, or interpreter, for whom the language signifies something; and third, there is the factor of the "something" referred to, the content signified.

All three aspects must be present in any genuine signification-situation. If, first, the language itself is missing, then, necessarily, this language cannot signify anything to anyone. When a person is directly confronted with an object or event, without the mediation of language, there is no signification-situation but, instead, a situation of "immediate presentation." If, second, there is no interpreter (or user-interpreter) present, then the language will fail to signify; it will be no more than one object (marks or sound-vibrations) among many others in our world. It is a mistake to suppose language to be "intrinsically" significant. Written marks or vocal noises are not significant if there is no one to whom they are the occasion of significance. Written marks *become* significant when an interpreter who "understands" them is supplied. This is not to say, of course, that language is "absolutely" non-significant if it is not significant *to me;* it is instead radically to question the notion of "absolute significance." If, finally, there is no content signified, no reference made to any actual or possible state of affairs, then again no signification-situation is established. It would be absurd, of course, to suggest that the signification-situation requires that the referent signified by the language always be *actual,* since this would confuse false statements (referring to no actual state of affairs) with non-significant ones. At the same time, a statement must point *beyond* itself if it is to signify; should it fail to point beyond itself but instead draw attention to itself *qua* language, a situation of immediate presentation would replace a signification-situation. It is helpful here to adopt C. W. Morris's distinction between the *designatum* of a statement, which is the possible state of affairs beyond itself to which a statement must refer if there is to be a signification-situation, and the *denotatum* of a statement, which is the actual state of affairs referred to if such there be. False assertions are thus significant if they have a designatum; they need not possess a denotatum as well. Frequently, as in fiction, statements occasion the signification-situation by referring to designata for which there exist no corresponding denotata.

It is possible, and for the sake of completeness it would be desirable, to show the applicability of these remarks concerning signification to non-verbal contexts—and even to the vast number of cases in which the "interpreter" of non-verbal signs is not a human being. But in order to avoid complicating issues any more than necessary, I shall restrict my attention to the highly specialized instance of signification wherein man, an interpreter overwhelmingly more gifted in the employment of free ideas than any other animal, uses language, a system of conventional signs (usually verbal) incomparably more flexible, subtle, and complex than any other means of signification.

The points of view from which this remarkable phenomenon may be approached correspond, as Morris points out, to the three essential elements of the signification-situation. First, language may be studied in terms of the endlessly fascinating relationships between the verbal signs themselves. This area of investigation, often called "syntactics," abstracts from the full signification-situation. It ignores both the referring function of language and the role of the interpreter in order to investigate more fully the "formal" properties of language. Formal logic, with its concern for tracing the systematic structures found within language and for elaborating rules of formation, transformation, implication, and equivalence, is most intimately associated with the syntactic dimension of language-theory.

Second, one may investigate language in terms of the relationship between language and the user-interpreter. Such a study, which I shall call "interpretics," will emphasize the forms of human activity that are associated with the employment of language, the purposes motivating its use, the effects it has on its interpreters, and like questions. Investigation of language in the interpretic dimension would no doubt overlap at many points with psychology, anthropology, and sociology.

Third, an approach to language may be made in terms of the relationship between language and its referent. A popular name for this field of investigation is "semantics." How does language refer? If it is successful in referring, how does it describe its referent? What, most crucially of all, are the criteria by which its reference and its description are to be judged "true" or "false"? Are all uses of language to be judged according to the same semantic rules? Since these questions are neither empirical nor purely formal, philosophical investigation of the semantic dimension of language, unlike either the syntactic or the interpretic dimensions, overlaps neither the formal nor the empirical disciplines.

While each of the three dimensions of language—syntactic, interpretic, and semantic—is an important area for intensive study, it must not be forgotten that each apart from the others is an abstraction. Language as a whole is not understood fully from the point of view of formal logic alone, as modern thinkers are increasingly coming to realize. But without stability on its syntactic dimension language could neither refer nor be of any use to an interpreter. Similarly, language cannot be exhaustively treated in terms of human behavior, although apart from the human beings, their needs, purposes, and responses, there would *be* no language. And in like respect, while no purely semantic approach to language can tell the whole tale of its nature and uses, discourse which is lacking in reference can lay no claim to a share in the logic of the signification-situation.

One of the major sources of confusion concerning the analysis of theological discourse is a failure to distinguish the three dimensions of the signification-situation as they arise in the full, concrete functioning of theological language. Some commentators fasten on the syntactic dimension and interpret everything from the point of view of logical entailments as though theological language were nothing more than a deductive logical system. J. L. Mackie's treatment of the problem of evil, for example, emphasizes the syntactic dimension to the exclusion of the rest.

Other thinkers dwell on interpretic considerations to the extent that system and reference are not recognized as a vital part of the logic of theological speech. Braithwaite, Hepburn, and others are guilty of this oversimplification, as are many other proponents of functional analysis, whose principles readily tempt one to devote one's attention too exclusively to the interpretic dimension of language.

Still others devote themselves so completely to questions concerning the possibility of meaningful—or truthful—reference for theological statements that all other issues are ignored. Unquestionably such semantic questions are of the utmost interest to theists and non-theists alike—and there is no doubt at all that this dimension has provoked many of the hottest controversies through the years —but a proper concern for semantic issues must not become obsessional, to the point that all other considerations are blotted out. Verificational analysis, with its central interest in the reference of language beyond itself to some state of affairs, risks falling into this error. Its definitive verification principle is itself a semantic rule for judging the success of language in referring; only those statements (other than tautologies) which can be shown to be relevant in principle to some sense-experience, we recall, are held on this criterion to be significant. The controversy over the falsifiability of theological discourse is an example of one type of concern for the semantic dimension of theological statements.

No one can justly condemn a given treatment of theological language solely because it fails to deal with all the dimensions of language which, in a complete analysis, would be essential. Each dimension deserves individual attention, and linguistic analysts have every right to specialize for particular purposes in areas of particular interest to them. But narrow emphases must be recognized for the academic abstractions they are. Any claim to a *full* understanding of theological discourse which ignores or treats inadequately one or more entire dimensions of the signification-situation is, to say the least, premature.

If theological language displays such a multi-dimensional logic, any adequate theory of theological language will doubtless make possible the synthesis of various valid insights which, alone, remain systematically abstract. Nothing in principle would seem to prevent our utilizing emphases drawn from the logics of analogy, obedience, and various philosophers to enrich our understanding of theological syntactics; nothing forces us to reject all the conclusions derived through functional analysis or from the logic of obedience concerning the dimension of theological interpretics; and nothing would rule out the possibility of learning something both from the logic of encounter and from verificational analysis in respect to the character of theism's semantic reference. We cannot for a moment relax our critical vigilance, but if our primary aim is full understanding, we shall gladly accept help from every quarter.

II

Beginning with the syntactic dimension of theological discourse, we must call once again on our distinction between the religious language of living faith and systematic language of academic theology. The syntactic rules by which these two forms of theological discourse are governed differ from one another even while they interact. Although we cannot hope to do more than start opening up a relatively untouched area of study in these concluding pages, we may at least note the direction which more comprehensive studies of theological syntactics may take.

The language of a living religious faith is judged for syntactic adequacy by reference to internal language-norms. For Christians, these language-norms are basically Scripture and Church traditions, creeds, and authoritative declarations. More accurately, in view of the fragmented condition of the Christian Church, the language-norms of living faith are those particular oral or written verbal standards which are, as MacIntyre rightly notes, simply "given" (so far as the syntactic dimension alone is concerned) as authoritative. The direct utterances of religious belief are syntactically correct in so far as they repeat the "faith of our fathers, living still." Compatibility with—more, re-expression of—the words of the Bible or the creeds is the essential syntactical demand placed on *religious* statements as distinguished from the statements of systematic theology. Compatibility of the various utterances of living faith with one another is, however, no part of the syntactic logic of this language. Frequently the incompatibilities which are apparent between many statements of living faith are denounced by the unsympathetic as "double-think," but such accusations are unfair. The canons of formal logic do not apply *between* the utterances which are the "protocol-statements" of religion. The primary syntactic relationship for the language of living faith is that of equivalence, not entailment; and the primary application of this relationship is between the words of the believer and the "given" paradigms of faithful talk, not between some of his words and other of his words, as would be the case in a deductive system.

The syntactic structure of systematic theological discourse, in contrast, is characterized in part by discoverable rules of entailment and equivalence between the statements comprising it. But modern philosophy is increasingly aware that there are a variety of kinds of such syntactic "rules," which are framed, as P. F. Strawson expresses it, "in the light of . . . our practice."[1] Let us briefly examine the case for this view. Some logicians suppose that the only logically important rules for implication, contradiction, and so on, are to be found in the operations of concepts so completely general as to be entirely devoid of reference to subject matter. "And," "not," "if . . . then," and "or" are so general that they can be used equally well with any content ("black *and* blue," "John *and* Mary," "I love you *and* you love me"), or with no particular content, without loss of the meaning important for logical operations. Logical rules of syntax of this kind, where descriptive content counts for nothing, we may call *formal* logic.

But logical theorists in recent years have come to recognize that other kinds of rules for implication, contradiction, and the like, play an important part in rational discourse. These are syntactical rules which are not irrelevant to the specific content being discussed, as are the rules of formal logic, but are openly dependent upon the definitions that establish inferences *within the language of a given subject matter*. In the language of the game of checkers, for example, the statement "It is permissible to jump your opponent's piece" *entails* "You are required to jump your opponent's piece." But such an entailment-rule does not have the complete generality associated with formal logic; in "the language of chess," for example, no such entailment holds. In ordinary language our speech is heavily dependent upon this non-formal (or, as we shall call them, "informal") kind of entailment and equivalence. We are justified in recognizing an explicit contradiction (given a unique reference for "John") between the statement "John is a mulatto" and the further statement "John's father is not a Negro and John's mother is not a Negro," on the basis of an informal equivalence between "X is a mulatto" and "X is the first-generation offspring of a pure-blooded Negro and a white person." As Gilbert Ryle puts it, "Not all strict inferences pivot on the recognized logical constants"[2] that can be formalized in symbolic logic. The study of both major kinds of syntactics, formal and informal, is proving to be of considerable importance for the understanding of language. To denounce "informal" syntactics as "bastard logic" or to sneer at formal logic as an "artificial appendix to the logic of ordinary language" is self-defeating and obscurantist. The formal and the "informal" logician are at work on different jobs.

The language of systematic theology exemplifies syntactic rules both of formal and of "informal" logic. Like the language of all other subjects, theological language relies on the formal logical constants to provide the rigid framework for its operations. "And" functions to conjoin expressions within theological discourse in the same manner as in any other statements. "Or" and "not," "some" and "all"—these retain their lofty irrelevance to the content of discussion. Without this common framework in formal logic, the language of systematic theology could neither be credited with any rational rigor nor even be understood.

But in addition to the operation of the formal constants within academic theological discourse, "informal" rules of inference provide this speech with its distinctive syntactic structure. One such rule, for example,[3] might be stated "If salvation is possible, then God cannot be merely a conditioned part of the world and subject to change." Another lays down the implication "If salvation is possible, then God cannot be completely apart from the world and unrelated to change." The formal logician might be tempted to symbolize "salvation is possible" by "S" and "God is involved in change" by "C," and then to derive an explicit contradiction from these entailment-rules: "S implies C and S implies not-C," "S" being given as a premise. The formal contradiction would be "C and not-C." But in this the formal logician oversteps himself. It is by no means clear that all expressions of the abstract form "C and not-C" are self-stultifying contradictions, though on the strictly formal level they undoubtedly are nothing more. The informal logician will recognize that even explicit formal contradictions are not necessarily always self-stultifying but sometimes may be occasions for growth in thought.

If, on an unpleasant day, I describe the weather by saying "It's raining and it's not," I am uttering a formal contradiction, but it may be the best possible characterization of the day. If it is, it will not be so merely because I use a form of words which seems to contradict itself but because the expression I use acts as an incentive to increased conceptual precision. Perhaps the English language is not yet equipped to indicate the more-than-drizzling but less-than-sprinkling condition of the atmosphere. The subject matter demands an increase in vocabulary, a more careful act of attention to what is the case. Again, "She's pretty and she's not," "He's likable and he's not" serve to suggest that further refinement of our concepts of "pretty" or "likable" is needed before an adequate non-paradoxical statement about him or her will be in order. Likewise the apparent contradiction "God is involved in change and he is not" is an indication that further investigation of our concepts of "involvement" and "change" are in order so that we may discover more precisely their logical powers for the inferences which, in theology, hinge on them.

Formal logic attains its precision and elegance by defining terms sharply—thus eliminating by fiat all vagueness from the concepts which it employs. Such a procedure is quite legitimate *if* one's aim is to construct a model language of syntactic rigor; but defenders of "informal" logic are right to protest when the truly vexing terms of theology and philosophy are at stake. These cannot be solved or dismissed arbitrarily. The heart of creative philosophical or systematic theological thought is precisely the elucidation of key concepts. Before a word may be accepted within a *formal* calculus, it must be pellucid, its entailment-rules already clearly determined; but if the *informal* logic of the crucial concepts of theology were clear to begin with, the assistance of formal logic would not be required. Judgment, imagination—even intuition—must go into the determination of the syntactic powers of every central theological concept before formal logical operations with it become profitable; it is precisely in this preliminary determination that the living issues lie.

Formal Logic may provide the exploratory Informal Logician with a compass by which to steer, but not with a course on which to steer and certainly not with rails to obviate steering. Where there is virgin forest, there can be no rails; where rails exist the jungle has long since been cleared.[4]

It is in this context that the logic of analogy may be appreciated; as laying down guiding rules for the further determination of fundamental theological concepts it offers considerable assistance to the systematic theologian in search of a more adequate syntactic structure for his language. Systematic theology—in contrast to the paradox-ridden "biblical" theology often supported by the logic of obedience—cannot rest in contradiction but improves and refines its concepts in a never-ending effort both to retain rational coherence and to respect the fundamental entailment and equivalence rules which distinguish its language from all others.

In returning once again to these fundamental "given" rules, which function within systematic theological discourse analogously to the axioms and postulates of other deductive systems, we recognize that the syntactic structure of academic theological language is not exclusively based upon the demands of systematic coherence. The axioms of academic theology are determined by the language of living faith, of which it is the reason-oriented explication. Systematic pronouncements, in turn, are often reflected after a time in the very creeds which judge the language of living faith! In this complex process of influence and counter-influence some of the most absorbing aspects of theological syntactics are to be found. As Ramsey and Crombie have noticed, the axioms of the systematic language of theology display a logical "oddness" which consequently characterizes the entire language of theism. Within systematic theological discourse, Crombie shows, this odd syntactic structure relates to the semantic dimension by clarifying the reference-range of theological statements both positively (suggesting the proper use of the term "God") and negatively (ruling out inappropriate objects of reference). Within the language of living faith, on the other hand, the function of the syntactical structure of theological discourse pertains to the interpretic dimension, perhaps as Ramsey describes, and certainly in many other ways. These fundamental syntactical features of theological discourse do not appear *ex nihilo,* therefore; but to examine their source and further functions it is necessary to leave the syntactic dimension for the interpretic and the semantic.

III

It is now clear, from prior discussion, that no understanding of theism is possible apart from a recognition of the interpretic functions of its language. It is often not so clear, however, that within this dimension we may distinguish two different aspects. One aspect of interpretics concerns the way in which language *affects* its interpreter; the second aspect deals with the circumstances under which the interpreter *uses* his language. We may label these two approaches, respectively, "passive" and "active" interpretics.

Those who emphasize "passive" interpretics are correct in pointing out the fact that all language affects those who hear it. In the very process of learning a language one becomes conditioned not merely to recognize the cognitive content of statements but also to react personally in certain ways to the words heard. Here is the psychological foundation for the "emotive" meaning which is so heavily stressed by verificational analysis. It is difficult to find a word—and more difficult to form a sentence—which is strictly "emotively neutral." Everyone realizes that "the same thing" may be said in very different ways, that listeners react to favorable or unfavorable emotive overtones associated with the words one uses.

"Mere choice of words" may turn a battle, decide a legacy, or hang a man.

The blanket term "emotive" conceals, however, the fundamental difference between two sorts of non-informational effect which language works on its interpreters. Where the emotive content of a word or phrase is one which has become connected with the language by a conventional process of association, there is present only what may be termed "reactive" significance. But language is capable not merely of eliciting reactions to superficial emotional associations habitually provoked by certain words but also of stirring many of the most fundamental personal depths in men to a response. Whereas we "react" to emotionally conditioned phrases, we "respond" to symbols which touch the springs of human motivation. Such symbols are invested with what I should like to call "responsive" significance.[5] To these symbols we do not need to be habituated to react in one way or another; we respond immediately. More accurately, the language we learn to use refers to things or events which are themselves the symbols demanding our response.

Far more needs to be said concerning reactive and responsive significance than would be possible here, but perhaps enough has been written to suggest an important distinction which has not been sufficiently noticed within what is usually called "emotive" meaning. To call responsive significance "emotive" would be to recognize its deep roots in the human personality and its capacity to influence human thought and behavior; but the "emotive" label is in danger of begging too many questions to be fully adequate. It is not clear that responsive significance must be entirely "non-cognitive"—we shall consider this issue in the next section of this chapter—but "emotive" and "non-cognitive" have, for better or for worse, become almost synonymous in modern philosophical parlance. Therefore we shall do well to be critical of the use of the term "emotive," which has itself become invested for many people with a strongly negative reactive significance!

Theological language, as countless philosophers have been at pains to point out, is rich in "emotive" meaning. But what, precisely, is meant by this observation? In part, no doubt, the terms of theological statements act upon their interpreters on the relatively superficial level of reactive significance. As evidence for this we need only notice the discomfort which people often feel, worshiping in a strange church, merely because the words are slightly different in the hymnal or prayer book. Or we may point to the reactive resistance occasioned by new translations of the Bible which may attempt to abandon words grown dear by habitual association.

In greater part, however, theological discourse is characterized by responsive significance. Its words deal with symbols of great potency. Christian language refers centrally to the Birth, the Baptism, the Cross, the Resurrection; the language of Judaism speaks of the crossing of the Red Sea, the imparting of the Covenant; and so on. Not the words or phrases themselves but the content of the words and phrases of theological speech possesses the greatest power to affect the interpreter of this language. Here is one source of the constant demand for more and better translations of the Bible, for more and better restatements of the *kerygma* for each generation. It is not the case that all responsive significance is religious, nor is all religious significance responsive, but much of what is most characteristic of theological meaning is best understood in these terms.

The language which affects an interpreter by means of its reactive and its responsive significance is also vitally instrumental in molding the thoughts of those who are served by it. As Wisdom points out, one's aptness to notice one or another pattern in the facts is profoundly affected by the concepts which one's language can express. So powerful is the influence of language upon the mind, indeed, that many psychologists and anthropologists agree that perceptions themselves may vary, *Gestalten* differ, among users of different languages. Where there is no word, thought will not be developed highly, if at all; and where clear thought is absent the mind tends not to notice data—however vivid to others—for which it has no ready conceptual categories.

We cannot rest content, however, with these considerations noted by "passive" interpretics. True as it is that the categories of language greatly mold one's concepts, that the words of language evoke one's reactions, and that the symbols expressed in language call up one's deep responses, it is also—and more fundamentally—true that language is a human product and cannot be understood apart from its source in human interests and activities. The categories, terms, and symbols of language have not been sheerly "given" (though syntactics correctly ignores this fact) but have a natural history in human purposes. "Thinking and speaking are part of life. They arise out of lived experience, and directly or indirectly they react upon it."[6] Human language is used; man is maker and ultimately master of his discourse. "Man the thinker and speaker is only one facet of man the purposeful."[7] If language imposes its categories, its reactive significance, and its responsive significance, it does not do so in the manner of an absolute tyrant. Only after having been formed in the womb of pre-linguistic social interests and activities does it seem to have a life of its own. And even this seeming independence is an illusion. Language is a human instrument as sensitive to shifts in non-linguistic interests and activities as is a smoothly functioning democratic government to fluctuations in public sentiment. The parallel is fairly good: In a democracy stability is preserved, public opinion is greatly influenced, by government policy and established media of communication, but final authority rests with the electors and, ultimately, with their individual interests and purposes. Similarly, established language-forms guide thought, emotion, and even perception to a considerable degree; but they are open to growth, through the addition of new concepts, and to the transformation of ancient categories as new experiences and preoccupations force themselves on the linguistic community. In the beginning, in this context, was not the word but the actor capable of speech; these abide then, word, thought, and purpose, and the greatest of these is purpose.

Theological language, like all forms of discourse, is the child of human purpose (whether or not this human purpose has a superhuman author and object is not here at issue), and it is the speech of an active society of language user-interpreters. The profound insight of the logic of obedience is to emphasize the unmistakable fact that the society of which theological language is the distinctive speech is the Church, broadly understood. It is this society of active human beings (dedicated, as Braithwaite and Hepburn clearly see, to a certain way of life) which preserves the syntactical criteria that provide theological speech with its distinctive formal character. It is this society which uses the language of living faith in its acts of public and private worship. It is this society which supports and demands the activity of systematic theology. Karl Barth exhibits his insight into this dimension of theological language by insisting that his writings be called "Church dogmatics."

In all this we must not forget that the activity of the community which employs theological discourse is itself motivated. In part, no doubt, this motivation is made up (as critics point out) of petty conservatism, respect for honored tradition, and the like. But more important, the activity of the Church in worship and speech is impelled by religious experience and by man's powerful need to find a place for himself within a coherent concept of the universe which does not violate his deepest sense of value. The experiences which motivate the theological language-using community may be variously described. Their place, as the logic of encounter rightly insists, is enormously important, but their function is not somehow to prove beyond question the existence of a deity; instead, they are primarily continuing incentives to worship, to service, and to self-commitment to the responsively rich religious symbols and the way of life which the Church enjoins. Despite the fact that so-called "encounters with God" cannot, as we have seen, prove the existence of any independent being who is the cause of these experiences, it is none the less true that the experiences which impel the Church to service and speech are not taken as mere experiences. Instead they are understood within a metaphysical world-view referring beyond the interpreter and his language. The activities of "worship" which we have noted as characteristic of the theological language-using society are radically misunderstood apart from reference to *belief* about the nature of reality beyond the acts and the actors themselves. Apart from the semantic reference of language, therefore, theological discourse lacks an essential dimension.

IV

On the basis of our discussion in earlier chapters it is apparent that theological discourse intends, at least, to refer to reality—to some state of affairs, to "facts" of some kind. As Ian Crombie puts it,

Christianity, as a human activity, involves much more than simply believing certain propositions about matters of fact, such as that there is a God, that He created this world, that He is our judge. But it does involve believing these things, and this believing is, in a sense, fundamental; not that it matters more than the other things that a Christian does, but that it is presupposed in the other things that he does, or in the manner in which he does them.[8]

Without the element of *belief in* the reality of a referent designated by theological language, the distinctively religious character of this speech is sought in vain. The syntactic character of theological discourse, as we saw, requires further explanation in terms of the society of language-using-and-interpreting agents, their purposes and activities, their attitudes and emotions. But these practices and feelings of the interpretic dimension attain the status of genuinely *religious* practices and feeling only when associated with beliefs, as Crombie insists, which have a reference. C. J. Ducasse remarks pungently,

> The beliefs are then for man what gives meaning to all the other aspects of his religion. Without the beliefs, he might go through the motions of it, but only as an automaton. To an observer of his outward behavior, he might still seem religious, but would in reality no more be so than a parrot that had been taught to recite the "Lord's Prayer," or an ape that had been taught to kneel and cross himself.[9]

It has also become clear that the sort of "facts" to which theological statements claim to have reference are not the same kind of facts which are discussed in the language of the empirical sciences. No straightforward experimental method for verifying or falsifying sentences claiming to state these "facts" seems to be available—or to be desired by those who use the sentences. The explanatory logic of the natural sciences, requiring expansibility, specificity, and regularity, is also inapplicable to these crucial religious "facts." Evidently theological discourse does not intend to refer merely to "natural" facts, if we take the "natural" (as Nowell-Smith suggests) to include whatever can be dealt with by the experimental methods and explanatory techniques of science. At the same time we have had occasion to question Hare's belief that the "supernatural" facts of religion are nothing but ordinary empirical facts regarded in an attitude of worship. There seems no escape from the conclusion that the intended semantic reference of theological discourse is to "metaphysical fact" of some kind.

"Facts," as both Hare and Wisdom point out, are never "given" apart from the minds which receive them. Ordinary "facts" of our everyday life are accepted as such because of their coherent place within the conceptual schema with which modern man relates himself to the world of common experience, though we usually ignore the vital role of mind in organizing even sense-experience into meaningful patterns of facts out of the "buzzing, blooming confusion" of bare sensation. What are judged "the facts" today are by no means identical to what were "the facts" a century, five centuries, three millennia ago. And we may expect that "the facts" of our generation will gradually and piecemeal give place to "the facts" of the future. Both "internal" conceptual refinement and "external" confrontation with experience that is difficult to deal with in terms of old concepts result in changes as to what are taken to be "the facts."

The "facts" of science, furthermore, are typically theories overwhelmingly confirmed by conceptually organized experience and by their key position within the elaborate theoretical schemata of the sciences. Here again "the facts" depend both on compatibility with experience and on deftness of theoretical formulation. Shortcomings on either side will in time demand that even "the facts" be reconsidered, though such revolutions in science are major undertakings and not frequent happenings.

When we speak of metaphysical "facts," therefore, we need not suppose that these are "given" independent of the creative powers of intelligence. On the contrary, the "facts" of metaphysics are supremely dependent on the conceptual activity of mind. The nature of metaphysics, I suggest, is *conceptual synthesis*. A metaphysical system is a construct of concepts designed to provide coherence for all "the facts" on the basis of a theoretical model drawn from among "the facts." A "metaphysical fact," therefore, is a concept which plays a key role within the system, without which the system would founder.

If this is the case, "metaphysical facts" are always facts relative to a specific metaphysical system. I readily accept this conclusion. "Space-time" is a metaphysical fact relative to Alexander's metaphysical conceptual synthesis; "duration" is a metaphysical fact relative to the schema of Bergson. But there is no cause for concern at this turn of the argument, because all facts of whatever kind are relative, in so far as they are known, to the system in which they play a key role. Metaphysical facts, in the last analysis, depend for their confirmation on the adequacy of the system in which they operate, but so must the facts of science ultimately rely on the validity of the entire scientific enterprise of which they are part.

To convince a Hindu mystic of a "fact of science" one must do more than perform an experiment before him.

Can metaphysical systems be judged *rationally* as to adequacy or inadequacy? Scientific systems are open to the possibility of falsification; scientific explanations are uncontroversially explanatory. There are applicable criteria for evaluating "better" or "worse" scientific hypotheses and explanations. Are any criteria in principle derivable for the extraordinarily inclusive conceptual syntheses of metaphysics?

Despite widespread negative answers to this question, I am increasingly coming around to the view that criteria can be found by which metaphysical systems can be graded. These grand syntheses, by attempting to unify and "make sense" out of ranges of ideas otherwise unrelated, aim at performing the function within the conceptual realm that the mental categories of perception perform in drawing meaning out of "buzzing, blooming confusion." They aim to provide, in our earlier terminology, explanations-B (of a different order from scientific explanations-A), within which scientific explanations may find a rationally satisfying context together with non-scientific principles of valuation. In so far as metaphysical systems have a definite function, then, they can be judged according to their success in fulfilling this function.

Both "internal" and "external" criteria become relevant for assessing the worth of a metaphysical conceptual synthesis.[10] Internally, a metaphysical system must pass the test of consistency: the presence of explicit logical contradictions within a conceptual schema destroys its integrity, undermines its meaningfulness, and violates the very quest for rational satisfaction that motivates it. But consistency is obviously a negative criterion. Though any metaphysical system which can be convicted of an explicit self-contradiction deserves swift discard, few major metaphysical syntheses are easily vulnerable to this charge. Consistency is a necessary but not a sufficient condition for the acceptance of a metaphysical system. Besides consistency, therefore, one must look for "coherence" in a conceptual scheme, especially where this scheme is of unlimited generality as in metaphysics. Since the role of the system is to provide unity in place of conceptual fragmentation, there can be no disconnection between the fundamental principles of the system. The model chosen for the metaphysical unification of thought must not itself be fragmented or permit of exceptions. A. N. Whitehead rightly complains of a fatal incoherence within the metaphysical system of Descartes, who never succeeded in providing a connection between his concepts of "matter" and "mind." The incoherence which poisons his entire metaphysical system becomes most glaringly obvious in his inability to account for the mind-body relationship. Such incoherence within the conceptual framework of a would-be "conceptual synthesis" is the mark of defeat; where there is incoherence there is no synthesis.

The first of the "external" criteria on which metaphysical systems may fruitfully be judged is applicability to experience. Like any conceptual schema, a metaphysical system is required to have relevance to experience, but not necessarily the *kind* of relevance (openness to falsification and the like) which scientific method demands. "Applicability" here means simply that a metaphysical synthesis— however beautifully consistent and flawlessly coherent—must be capable of illuminating *some* experience naturally and without distortion. But it is obvious that this requirement may be met without our being required to approve the system. Perhaps some conceptual syntheses of unlimited theoretical generality are applicable—"ring true"—only to narrow ranges of experience. Some of Sartre's critics might delightedly be found to maintain that his and some other existentialists' metaphysical views are applicable only to the experience of "the morning after," when talk of the "hostile pressure of obscenely inert being" may become highly illuminating! Applicability alone, like consistency alone, is not enough. A conceptual synthesis must not only be applicable to some experience which it interprets; it must (much more demandingly) be adequate to *all* possible experience, if it is to succeed in being of unlimited generality; that is, it must show all experience to be interpreted without oversight, distortion, or "explaining away" on the basis of its key concepts.

To say that theological discourse refers to "metaphysical fact" is equivalent to asserting that theological language *on its semantic dimension* functions as metaphysical language. It seems to me that, roughly speaking, this is the case. The language of living religious faith is not used, of course, for the sake of a metaphysical explanation-B; but questions of motivation (an interpretic category) are irrelevant to semantic considerations. Theological speech projects a model of immense responsive significance, drawn from "the facts," as the key to its conceptual synthesis. This model, for theism, is made up of the "spiritual" characteristics of personality: will, purpose, wisdom, love, and the like. For Christianity, more specifically, the conceptual model consists in the creative, self-giving, personal love of Jesus Christ. In this model is found the only literal meaning which these terms, like "creative," "personal," and "love," can have in the Christian vocabulary. All the concepts of the Christian are organized and synthesized in relation to this model. The efforts of systematic theology are bent to explicating the consistency and coherence of the synthesis built on this model of "God" as key concept. Christian preaching is devoted to pointing out the applicability of this conceptual synthesis to common experiences of life. And Christian apologetics struggles to show that the synthesis organized around this model is adequate to the unforced interpretation of all experience, including suffering and evil. It is not my purpose here to evaluate Christianity in particular or theism in general as to its success in these endeavors; my task has been simply to display accurately the logical anatomy of the process.

One final consideration remains. Metaphysical systems are conceptual syntheses, but they are conceptual syntheses which are considered to be grounded in and somehow faithful to reality. The metaphysician and the theologian-as-metaphysician insist that their syntheses have *ontological* bearing.

Religious thinking may well have other concerns besides the epistemological question of the relation of our ideas to reality beyond ourselves. But here, if anywhere, this question cannot be avoided, since religion loses its nerve when it ceases to believe that it expresses in some way truth about our relation to a reality beyond ourselves which ultimately concerns us.[11]

In what respect can theological statements claim to be *true* to reality? There is no longer any question of literal description, since, as we have seen, terms derived from contexts of limited generality cannot without distortion be applied in contexts of unlimited generality. If words are drawn from human experience and used concerning "ultimate reality," it will not be appropriate to expect a "picturing" relationship between language and referent. But if language literally based on certain models of great responsive depth found within human experience is capable not only of synthesizing our concepts in a coherent manner but also of illuminating our experience—moral experience, sense experience, aesthetic experience, religious experience—we may ask *why* this happens to be the case. And if some models are capable of providing greater coherence and adequacy than others, we may begin to suspect that this tells us something not only about the models but also about what reality is like: reality is of such a character that a metaphysical system based on model X is more capable of interpreting our experience and unifying our ideas than is a metaphysical system based on model Y. "Why from some features of our experience rather than others do metaphysical arguments spring up? The answer to that question would be the ultimate metaphysical answer."[12] Theism is founded on the belief that reality is such that the metaphysical models of personal activity will best survive any tests which may be demanded. This is perhaps what Crombie meant when he stated that "the more we try to understand the world in the light of this image, the better our understanding of the world becomes."

But *theological* statements are not the only ones which provide a possible model for the oblique understanding of the nature of things. Many rival conceptual syntheses are urged from different quarters. All, including theism, suffer apparent weakness; each, including theism, promises that continued refinement plus further experience will reveal that *it* best survives the "truth-criteria" of metaphysics. In the meanwhile, one is left to choose. There is no question of remaining aloof, taking no position on the character of reality. The poised and tentative posture is the natural one for cloistered thought; it is an impossible one for life. Every sane disposition for behavior is based on what is thought to be the case; every "forced option" which life thrusts on one has profound implications for one's implicit (or explicit) choice of a model in terms of which to conceive the ultimately real. Agnosticism of the mind in these matters may be cultivated among a narrow group of would-be purists, but daily challenges to action—where even inaction may be a culpable choice—make agnosticism in life an absurdity. And the choices which one does make, whether to worship a God of love or to refrain from it, whether to treat others as "means only" or in some other way, and so on, have their influence on the mind. In any but the most disintegrated personality, these choices will have a pattern of at least some stability; and study of this pattern can often disclose what model a man unconsciously has adopted as most true to reality.

Then "agnosticism" becomes a bland mask covering an uncritical practical decision to accept one or another metaphysical view: perhaps it will be the view that "God the Father of Jesus Christ" is most real, or, more likely, it will be the view that "quanta of energy without purpose or intrinsic value" provide the best model for this reality. A decision that goes beyond the security of sufficient reason is in any case required; and by pretending not to recognize the language of this decision—which many Christians call "the leap of faith"—one is denying himself the right to look before (and after) he leaps.

SUGGESTIONS FOR FURTHER READING

Allen, E. L. "The Arguments for God's Existence," *The Congregational Quarterly*, Vol. XXX, 1952.

————. "The Great Argument," *The Expository Times*, Vol. LVIII, 1947.

————. "Natural Theology in Karl Barth," *The Congregational Quarterly*, Vol. XXV, 1947.

————. "The New Orthodoxy and the Contemporary Mood," *The Congregational Quarterly*, Vol. XXVIII, 1950.

Ayer, A. J. *Language, Truth and Logic*. London: Victor Gollancz, Ltd., 1936. Second edition, 1946.

————, and others. *The Revolution in Philosophy*. London: Macmillan and Company, Ltd., 1957.

Baillie, D. M. *God Was in Christ*. London: Faber and Faber, Ltd., 1948.

Barnes, Winston H. F. *The Philosophical Predicament*. London: Adam and Charles Black, 1950.

Barth, Karl. *The Doctrine of the Word of God*. Translated by G. T. Thompson. Edinburgh: T. and T. Clark, 1936.

————. *The Knowledge of God and the Service of God*. Translated by J. L. M. Haire and I. Henderson. London: Hodder and Stoughton, 1938.

Bodkin, Maud. *Studies of Type-Images in Poetry, Religion, and Philosophy*. London: Oxford University Press, 1951.

Braithwaite, R. B. *An Empiricist's View of the Nature of Religious Belief*. Cambridge: Cambridge University Press, 1955.

Broad, C. D. *Religion, Philosophy and Psychical Research*. London: Routledge and Kegan Paul, Ltd., 1953.

Brown, James. *Subject and Object in Modern Theology*. London: SCM Press, Ltd., 1955.

Camfield, F. W. *The Collapse of Doubt*. London: Lutterworth Press, 1945.

Campbell, C. A. *On Selfhood and Godhood*. London: George Allen and Unwin, Ltd., 1957.

Casserley, J. V. Langmead. *The Christian in Philosophy*. London: Faber and Faber, Ltd., 1949.

Coates, J. B. "God and the Positivists," *The Hibbert Journal*, Vol. L, 1952.

Cocks, H. F. Lovell. *By Faith Alone*. London: James Clarke and Company, Ltd., 1943.

Copleston, F. C. *Aquinas*. Harmondsworth, Middlesex: Penguin Books, 1955.

———. *Contemporary Philosophy*. London: Burns and Oates, 1956.

———. "Existentialism and Religion," *The Dublin Review*, Vol. 220, No. 440, 1947.

———. "The Flight from Metaphysics," *The Month*, Vol. CLXXXV, 1948.

Corbishley, T. "Do the Mystics Know?" *The Hibbert Journal*, Vol. L, 1951.

Cox, David. "A Note on 'Meeting,' " *Mind*, Vol. LX, 1951.

———. "The Significance of Christianity," *Mind*, Vol. LIX, 1950.

Cunliffe-Jones, H. *The Authority of the Biblical Revelation*. London: James Clarke and Company, Ltd., 1945.

Davies, Rupert E. *The Problem of Authority in the Continental Reformers*. London: The Epworth Press, 1946.

Dickie, Edgar P. *God Is Light*. London: Hodder and Stoughton, 1953.

———. "Religious Experience: Its Validity," *Religion in Life*, Vol. VI, No. 4, 1937.

Dillistone, F. W. *Christianity and Symbolism*. London: Collins, 1955.

Ducasse, C. J. *A Philosophical Scrutiny of Religion*. New York: The Ronald Press Company, 1953.

Emmet, Dorothy M. *The Nature of Metaphysical Thinking*. London: Macmillan and Company, Ltd., 1945.

———. " 'Reason' in Recent Theological Discussion," *The Political Quarterly*, Vol. 26, 1955.

Evans, J. L. "On Meaning and Verification," *Mind*, Vol. LXII, 1953.

Ewing, A. C. "Religious Assertions in the Light of Contemporary Philosophy," *Philosophy*, Vol. XXXII, No. 122, July 1957.

Faith and Logic. Edited by Basil Mitchell. London: George Allen and Unwin, Ltd., 1957.

Farmer, H. H. *Revelation and Religion*. London: Nisbet and Company, 1954.

Farrer, Austin. "An English Appreciation," in *Kerygma and Myth, A Theological Debate*. Edited by Hans Werner Bartsch. Translated by Reginald H. Fuller. London: SPCK, 1953.

———. *Finite and Infinite*. Westminster: Dacre Press, 1943.

———. *The Glass of Vision*. Westminster: Dacre Press, 1948.

———. "The Queen of the Sciences," *The Twentieth Century*, Vol. CLVII, 1955.

Ferré, Frederick. "Is Language about God Fraudulent?" *The Scottish Journal of Theology*, Vol. 12, No. 4, December 1959.

Flew, Antony. "Philosophy and Language," *The Philosophical Quarterly*, Vol. 5, 1955.

——— (ed.). *Logic and Language*. Oxford: Basil Blackwell, First Series, 1951. Second Series, 1955.

———, and Hepburn, Ronald. "Problems of Perspective," *The Plain View*, 1955.

——— (ed.), and MacIntyre, Alasdair (ed.). *New Essays in Philosophical Theology*. London: SCM Press, Ltd., 1955.

Fraser, Ian M. "Theology and Action," *The Scottish Journal of Theology*, Vol. 2, 1949.

Gilkey, Langdon. *Maker of Heaven and Earth*. New York: Doubleday and Company, Inc., 1959.

Glasgow, W. D. "Cox: The Significance of Christianity: A Note," *Mind*, Vol. LX, 1951.

———. "Knowledge of God," *Philosophy*, Vol. XXXII, No. 122, July 1957.

Grensted, L. W. "The Changing Background of Theological Studies," *Bulletin of the John Ryland Library*, Vol. 37, No. 1, 1954.

Hall, W. Arnold. "Religious Experience as a Court of Appeal," *The Hibbert Journal*, Vol. LIII, 1955.

Hartland-Swann, John. "What Is Theology?" *Philosophy*, Vol. XXIX, 1954.

Hawkins, D. J. B. *The Essentials of Theism*. London: Sheed and Ward, 1949.

———. "Inference in Natural Theology," *The Church Quarterly Review*, Vol. CL, 1950.

———. "On the Demonstration of God's Existence," Part One, *The Downside Review*, Vol. LXIV, 1946.

———. Review of E. L. Mascall's *Existence and Analogy*, *The Church Quarterly Review*, Vol. CXLIX, 1950.

———. "What Do the Proofs of the Existence of God Purport to Do?" *The Clergy Review*, Vol. XXXVII, 1952.

Heinemann, F. H. "Man the Believing Animal," *The Hibbert Journal*, Vol. LIII, 1954.

Henderson, Ian. *Myth in the New Testament*. London: SCM Press, Ltd., 1952.

Hendry, G. S. "The Exposition of Holy Scripture," *The Scottish Journal of Theology*, Vol. 1, 1948.

Hepburn, Ronald W. *Christianity and Paradox*. London: Watts, 1958.

Hick, John. *Faith and Knowledge*. Ithaca, N.Y.: Cornell University Press, 1957.

Hodges, H. A. *Languages, Standpoints and Attitudes*. London: Oxford University Press, 1953.

————. "What Is to Become of Philosophical Theology?" *Contemporary British Philosophy.* Edited by H. D. Lewis. London: George Allen and Unwin, Ltd., 1956.

Hume, David. *Dialogues Concerning Natural Religion.* Edited by Norman Kemp Smith. London: Thomas Nelson and Sons, Ltd., 1935.

Inge, W. R. "Liberal Christianity," *The Hibbert Journal,* Vol. XLIX, 1951.

————. *Mysticism in Religion.* London: Hutchinson's University Library, undated.

————. "Theism," *Philosophy,* Vol. XXIII, 1948.

James, William. "The Sentiment of Rationality," *Essays in Pragmatism.* Edited by Alburey Castell. New York: Hafner Publishing Company, 1948.

Jenkins, Daniel T. *The Nature of Catholicity.* London: Faber and Faber, Ltd., 1942.

————. *Tradition and the Spirit.* London: Faber and Faber, Ltd., 1951.

Jones, O. Rogers. "The Challenge of a Contemporary Philosophy to Religion," *The Hibbert Journal,* Vol. LIII, 1955.

Knight, Marcus. "Religion and Language," *The Spectator,* October 17, 1947.

Leon, Philip. "An Existentialist 'Proof of the Existence of God,' " *The Hibbert Journal,* Vol. LI, 1952.

————. "The Meaning of Religious Propositions," *The Hibbert Journal,* Vol. LIII, 1955.

Lewis, H. D. "The Cognitive Factor in Religious Experience," *Proceedings of the Aristotelian Society,* Supplementary Vol. XXIX, 1955.

————. "What Is Theology?" *Philosophy,* Vol. XXVII, 1952.

Lillie, William. "The Preacher and the Critic," *The Scottish Journal of Theology,* Vol. 6, 1953.

Logic and Language. Edited by A. G. N. Flew. Oxford: Basil Blackwell, First Series, 1951. Second Series, 1955.

Loudon, R. Stuart. "The Ministry of the Word," *The Scottish Journal of Theology,* Vol. 2, 1949.

Lunn, Arnold. "Miracles—The Scientific Approach," *The Hibbert Journal,* Vol. XLVIII, 1950.

MacIntyre, Alasdair (ed.). *Metaphysical Beliefs.* London: SCM Press, Ltd., 1957.

————, and Flew, Antony (ed.). See under Flew, Antony.

Mackie, J. L. "Evil and Omnipotence," *Mind,* Vol. LXIV, 1955.

Macquarrie, John. *An Existentialist Theology.* London: SCM Press, Ltd., 1955.

Mascall, E. L. *Existence and Analogy.* London: Longmans, Green and Company, 1949.

————. *He Who Is.* London: Longmans, Green and Company, 1943.

————. *Words and Images*. London: Longmans, Green and Company, 1957.

Masterman, Margaret. "Belief Without Strain," *The Twentieth Century*, Vol. CLVII, 1955.

————. "Linguistic Philosophy and Dogmatic Theology," *Theology*, Vol. LIV, 1951.

————. "The Philosophy of Language, or the Study of Framework," *Theology*, Vol. LIV, 1951.

————. "What Is Philosophy Nowadays?" *Theology*, Vol. LIV, 1951.

Matthews, W. R. "The Aims and Scope of the Philosophy of Religion," *Journal of the Transactions of the Victoria Institute*, Vol. LXXXIV, 1952.

————. "Do We Need a Philosophy of Religion?" *The Hibbert Journal*, Vol. XLIII, 1945.

McConnochie, John. "The Uniqueness of the Word of God," *The Scottish Journal of Theology*, Vol. 1, No. 2, 1948.

McIntyre, John. "Analogy," *The Scottish Journal of Theology*, Vol. 12, No. 1, March 1959.

————. *St. Anselm and His Critics*. Edinburgh: Oliver and Boyd, 1954.

McPherson, Thomas. "The Argument from Design," *Philosophy*, Vol. XXXII, No. 122, July 1957.

————. "The Existence of God," *Mind*, Vol. LIX, 1950.

Metaphysical Beliefs. Edited by A. MacIntyre. London: SCM Press, Ltd., 1957.

Mitchell, Basil (ed.). *Faith and Logic*. London: George Allen and Unwin, Ltd., 1957.

Morris, C. W. *Foundations of the Theory of Signs*. Chicago: The University of Chicago Press, 1938.

New Essays in Philosophical Theology. Edited by A. G. N. Flew and Alasdair MacIntyre. London: SCM Press, Ltd., 1955.

The Nature of Metaphysics. Edited by D. F. Pears. London: Macmillan and Company, Ltd., 1957.

Paton, H. J. *The Modern Predicament*. London: George Allen and Unwin, Ltd., 1955.

Pears, D. F. (ed.). *The Nature of Metaphysics*. London: Macmillan and Company, Ltd., 1957.

Pontifex, Mark. *The Existence of God*. London: Longmans, Green and Company, 1947.

————, and Trethowan, Illtyd. *The Meaning of Existence*. London: Longmans, Green and Company, 1953.

Quine, W. V. O. "Two Dogmas of Empiricism," *The Philosophical Review*, Vol. XL, 1951.

Ramsey, Ian T. *Miracles, an Exercise in Logical Mapwork*. Oxford: Clarendon Press, 1952.

————. *Religious Language*. London: SCM Press, Ltd., 1957.

Raven, Charles E. *Natural Religion and Christian Theology*. Cambridge: Cambridge University Press, 1953.

Reid, Arnaud. "Religion, Science and Other Modes of Knowledge," *The Hibbert Journal*, Vol. LIV, 1955.

The Revolution in Philosophy. A. J. Ayer and others. London: Macmillan and Company, Ltd., 1957.

Richardson, A. *Christian Apologetics*. London: SCM Press, Ltd., 1947.

Riddell, J. G. "A Question of Words," *The Scottish Journal of Theology*, Vol. 1, 1948.

Robinson, N. H. G. *Faith and Duty*. London: Victor Gollancz, Ltd., 1950.

————. "Karl Barth's Empiricism," *The Hibbert Journal*, Vol. XLIX, 1951.

Russell, Bertrand. *An Inquiry into Meaning and Truth*. London: George Allen and Unwin, Ltd., 1940.

————. Introduction to Wittgenstein's *Tractatus Logico-Philosophicus*. London: Routledge and Kegan Paul, Ltd., 1922.

Ryle, Gilbert. *Dilemmas*. Cambridge: Cambridge University Press, 1954.

————. "Ordinary Language," *The Philosophical Review*, Vol. LXII, 1953.

Smethurst, Arthur F. *Modern Science and Christian Beliefs*. London: James Nisbet and Company, Ltd., 1955.

Stace, W. T. "Positivism," *Mind*, Vol. LIII, 1944.

Stevenson, Charles. *Ethics and Language*. New Haven: Yale University Press, 1944.

Strawson, P. F. *Introduction to Logical Theory*. London: Methuen and Company, Ltd., 1952.

Sutton, C. W. H. "Philosophy and Religion," *Philosophy*, Vol. XXVI, 1951.

Torrance, T. F. "Faith and Philosophy," *The Hibbert Journal*, Vol. XLVII, 1949.

————. "History and Reformation," *The Scottish Journal of Theology*, Vol. 4, 1951.

————. Review of Warfield's *The Inspiration and Authority of the Bible*, *The Scottish Journal of Theology*, Vol. 7, 1954.

————. "A Study in New Testament Communication," *The Scottish Journal of Theology*, Vol. 3, 1950.

————, and Reid, J. K. S. Editorial introducing the first number of *The Scottish Journal of Theology*, Vol. 1, 1948.

Trethowan, Dom Illtyd. *Certainty, Philosophical and Theological*. Westminster: Dacre Press, 1948.

————. "Do We Infer God's Existence?" *The Church Quarterly Review,* Vol. CL, 1950.

————. *An Essay in Christian Philosophy.* London: Longmans, Green and Company, 1954.

————. "How Do We Demonstrate God's Existence?" *The Downside Review,* Vol. LXIV, 1946.

————. "On the Demonstration of God's Existence," Part Two, *The Downside Review,* Vol. LXIV, 1946.

————. "The Problem of Supernatural Knowledge," *The Dublin Review,* Vol. 218, No. 436, 1946.

Turner, Vincent. "Preliminaries to Theism," *The Dublin Review,* Vol. 225, No. 450, 1951.

Urmson, J. O. *Philosophical Analysis.* Oxford: The Clarendon Press, 1956.

————. "Some Questions Concerning Validity," *Revue Internationale de Philosophie,* Tome VII, 1953.

Urquhart, W. S. "The Status of the Theologian in Philosophy," *The Expository Times,* Vol. LX, 1949.

Wallace, Ronald S. *Calvin's Doctrine of the Word and Sacrament.* Edinburgh: Oliver and Boyd, 1953.

————. "The Parable and the Preacher," *The Scottish Journal of Theology,* Vol. 2, 1949.

Watkin, E. I. "Consistent Empiricism," *The Hibbert Journal,* Vol. LI, 1952.

Webb, C. C. J. *Religious Experience.* London: Humphrey Milford, 1945.

Whitehead, A. N. *Process and Reality.* New York: Humanities Press, 1929.

Whitely, C. H. "The Cognitive Factor in Religious Experience," *Proceedings of the Aristotelian Society,* Supplementary Vol. XXIX, 1955.

Winch, Peter. "Contemporary British Philosophy and Its Critics," *Universities,* Vol. X, No. 1, 1955.

Wisdom, John. *Philosophy and Psychoanalysis.* Oxford: Blackwell, 1953.

Wittgenstein, Ludwig. *Philosophical Investigations.* Translated by G. E. M. Anscombe. Oxford: Basil Blackwell, 1953.

————. *Tractatus Logico-Philosophicus.* London: Routledge and Kegan Paul, Ltd., 1922.

Wren-Lewis, John. "Modern Philosophy and the Doctrine of the Trinity," *The Philosophical Quarterly,* Vol. 5, No. 20, 1955.

Zuurdeeg, Willem F. *An Analytical Philosophy of Religion.* Nashville: Abingdon Press, 1958.

NOTES

(For bibliographical details see Suggestions for Further Reading)

Chapter 1. The "Family Background" of Linguistic Philosophy

1. Flew, "Philosophy and Language," *Philosophical Quarterly*, p. 21.
2. Wittgenstein, *Philosophical Investigations*, p. 32e.
3. Wittgenstein, *Tractatus Logico-Philosophicus*, 4.1121.
4. *Ibid.*, 4.111.
5. Urmson, *Philosophical Analysis*, p. 116.
6. Ryle, Introduction, *The Revolution in Philosophy*, p. 8.
7. Evans, "On Meaning and Verification," p. 8.
8. Wittgenstein, *Tractatus*, 3.3.
9. Ryle, *The Revolution in Philosophy*, p. 10.
10. *Ibid.*, p. 4.
11. Ryle, "Systematically Misleading Expressions," *Logic and Language*, First Series.
12. For some examples see my article, "Is Langauge about God Fraudulent?" *The Scottish Journal of Theology*, especially pp. 337–342.
13. A. J. Ayer, *Language, Truth and Logic*, p. 52.

Chapter 2. The Logic of Verificational Analysis

1. Ayer, *Language, Truth and Logic*, pp. 59–60.
2. Wittgenstein, *Tractatus Logico-Philosophicus*, 6.11.
3. Ayer, *Language, Truth and Logic*, p. 79.
4. *Ibid.*, p. 86.
5. Bertrand Russell in the "Introduction" to Wittgenstein's *Tractatus Logico-Philosophicus*, p. 8.
6. This formulation is one of a number of semi-traditional slogans which might be offered at this point, a formulation interestingly discussed by Professor John Wisdom in "Metaphysics and Verification," reprinted from *Mind* in his *Philosophy and Psychoanalysis*. It should not be mistaken for a full statement of the principle of verification, which has passed through innumerable variant forms and is therefore not discussed in all its complexity in this introductory chapter.
7. Ayer, *Language, Truth and Logic*, p. 68.
8. *Ibid.*, p. 36.
9. Cf. Friedrich Waismann, "Verifiability," *Proceedings of the Aristotelian Society*, reprinted with alterations in *Logic and Language*, edited by Antony Flew.
10. Urmson, *Philosophical Analysis*, pp. 102–103.

Chapter 3. The "Elimination" of Theological Discourse

1. Ayer, *Language, Truth and Logic*, p. 115.
2. McPherson, "The Argument from Design," *Philosophy*, p. 228.

3. Ayer, *Language, Truth and Logic*, p. 118.

4. Alasdair MacIntyre, "Visions," *New Essays in Philosophical Theology,* edited by Antony Flew and Alasdair MacIntyre (London: SCM Press Ltd.; New York: The Macmillan Company, 1955), pp. 255–256. This quotation and all others from the same book are used by special permission of the publishers.

5. Ayer, *Language, Truth and Logic,* p. 120.

6. *Ibid.,* p. 119.

7. MacIntyre, "Visions," *New Essays in Philosophical Theology,* pp. 257–258.

8. *Ibid.,* p. 258.

9. McPherson, "The Argument from Design," p. 228.

10. Patrick Nowell-Smith, "Miracles," *New Essays in Philosophical Theology,* p. 251.

11. Mackie, "Evil and Omnipotence," *Mind,* p. 200.

12. *Ibid.,* p. 202.

13. *Ibid.,* p. 204.

14. *Ibid.,* pp. 205–206.

15. *Ibid.,* p. 209.

16. *Ibid.*

17. J. N. Findlay, "Can God's Existence Be Disproved?" *New Essays in Philosophical Theology,* p. 48.

18. *Ibid.*

19. *Ibid.,* p. 51.

20. *Ibid.,* p. 52.

21. *Ibid.,* pp. 54–55.

22. Flew, "Theology and Falsification," *New Essays in Philosophical Theology,* p. 96.

23. *Ibid.,* p. 97.

24. *Ibid.*

25. *Ibid.,* p. 98.

26. *Ibid.,* pp. 98–99.

27. Bernard Williams, "Tertullian's Paradox," *New Essays in Philosophical Theology,* p. 187.

28. *Ibid.,* p. 204.

29. *Ibid.,* pp. 208–209.

30. *Ibid.,* p. 209.

31. McPherson, "Religion and the Inexpressible," *New Essays in Philosophical Theology,* p. 133.

32. *Ibid.*

33. *Ibid.,* p. 139.

34. Cox, "The Significance of Christianity," *Mind,* p. 210.

35. *Ibid.,* p. 211.

36. *Ibid.*

37. *Ibid.,* p. 212.

38. *Ibid.,* p. 215.

39. *Ibid.,* p. 216.

40. *Ibid.*

41. *Ibid.*

42. *Ibid.,* p. 218.

43. *Ibid.,* p. 217.

44. McPherson, "The Existence of God," *Mind,* p. 547.

45. Cox, "A Note on 'Meeting,' " *Mind*, pp. 259–261.
46. McPherson, "The Existence of God," p. 545.
47. Glasgow, "Cox: The Significance of Christianity: A Note," *Mind*, p. 101.

Chapter 4. The Limits of Verificational Analysis

1. Cf. Stevenson, *Ethics and Language*. Chap. IX.
2. James, "The Sentiment of Rationality," *Essays in Pragmatism*, edited by Alburey Castell.
3. Wisdom, "Philosophical Perplexity," *Philosophy and Psychoanalysis*, p. 50.
4. *Ibid.*, p. 41.
5. *Ibid.*, p. 178.
6. A. C. A. Rainer (Windsor), Reply to Findlay's "Can God's Existence Be Disproved?" *New Essays in Philosophical Theology*, p. 68.
7. Basil Mitchell, "Theology and Falsification," *New Essays in Philosophical Theology*, p. 105.
8. Hare, *New Essays in Philosophical Theology*, p. 100.
9. Crombie, *New Essays in Philosophical Theology*, p. 124.
10. Hick, *Faith and Knowledge*, pp. 155–156.
11. *Ibid.*, p. 161.
12. Hare, "Religion and Morals," *Faith and Logic*, p. 177.
13. Cf. my "Is Language about God Fraudulent?" especially pp. 351–360.

Chapter 5. The Logic of Functional Analysis

1. Wittgenstein, *Philosophical Investigations*, p. 8e.
2. *Ibid.*, pp. 11e–12e.
3. *Ibid.*, p. 94e.
4. Evans, "On Meaning and Verification," p. 18.
5. Wittgenstein, *Philosophical Investigations*, p. 126e.
6. *Ibid.*, p. 128e.
7. *Ibid.*, p. 132e.
8. J. L. Austin, "Other Minds," *Logic and Language*, Second Series.
9. Ryle, "Ordinary Language," *The Philosophical Review*, pp. 174–175.
10. Flew, *Logic and Language*, Second Series, p. 9.
11. *Ibid.*, p. 9 n.
12. Evans, "On Meaning and Verification," p. 16.
13. *Ibid.*, p. 17.
14. Wittgenstein, *Philosophical Investigations*, p. 19e.
15. *Ibid.*, p. 51e.
16. See Findlay, "Time: A Treatment of Some Puzzles," *Logic and Language*, First Series, pp. 42 ff., for a modern treatment of these ponderings along functional analyst lines.

Chapter 6. The Logic of Analogy

1. Casserley, *The Christian in Philosophy*, p. 83.
2. Mascall, *Existence and Analogy*, p. 87.
3. Farrer, *Finite and Infinite*, p. 88.
4. Mascall, *Existence and Analogy*, p. 102.
5. *Ibid.*, p. 104.
6. Hawkins, *The Essentials of Theism*, p. 95.

7. Mascall, *Existence and Analogy,* p. 108.
8. *Ibid.,* p. 102.
9. Emmet, *The Nature of Metaphysical Thinking,* p. 180.
10. Cf. Hawkins, *The Essentials of Theism,* especially Chap. VI.
11. Copleston, "The Meaning of the Terms Predicated of God," *Contemporary Philosophy,* p. 96.

Chapter 7. The Logic of Obedience

1. Torrance, "Faith and Philosophy," *The Hibbert Journal,* p. 237.
2. *Ibid.*
3. *Ibid.,* p. 241.
4. *Ibid.,* p. 242.
5. *Ibid.,* p. 243.
6. *Ibid.*
7. *Ibid.,* pp. 243–244.
8. *Ibid.,* p. 244 (italics added).
9. *Ibid.,* p. 241.
10. Torrance, "History and Reformation," *The Scottish Journal of Theology,* p. 284.
11. Hendry, "The Exposition of Holy Scripture," *The Scottish Journal of Theology,* p. 36.
12. Torrance, review of Warfield, *The Scottish Jornal of Theology,* p. 106.
13. Hendry, "The Exposition of Holy Scripture," p. 36.
14. Barth, *The Doctrine of the Word of God,* p. 2.
15. *Ibid.,* pp. 2–3.
16. *Ibid.,* p. 3.
17. Torrance and J. K. S. Reid, editorial introducing the first number of *The Scottish Journal of Theology,* p. 3.
18. Fraser, "Theology and Action," *The Scottish Journal of Theology,* p. 411.
19. *Ibid.,* p. 415.
20. *Ibid.,* p. 412.
21. *Ibid.,* p. 413.
22. *Ibid.,* p. 416.
23. Jenkins, *Tradition and the Spirit,* p. 186.
24. Wallace, *Calvin's Doctrine of the Word and Sacrament,* p. 83.
25. Hendry, "The Exposition of Holy Scripture," p. 38.
26. Robinson, "Karl Barth's Empiricism," *The Hibbert Journal,* p. 365.
27. *Ibid.*
28. Cocks, *By Faith Alone,* p. 74.
29. Torrance, review of Warfield, p. 107.
30. Camfield, *The Collapse of Doubt,* pp. 45–46.
31. Hepburn, "Poetry and Religious Belief," *Met physical Beliefs,* p. 159.
32. *Ibid.,* p. 106.
33. Paton, *The Modern Predicament,* p. 58.
34. *Ibid.,* p. 54.

Chapter 8. The Logic of Encounter

1. Dickie, *God Is Light,* p. 37.
2. Farmer, *Revelation and Religion,* p. 42.
3. *Ibid.,* p. 50.

4. *Ibid.*
5. *Ibid.*, p. 58.
6. *Ibid.*, p. 70.
7. Urquhart, "The Status of the Theologian in Philosophy," *The Expository Times*, p. 158.
8. Inge, *Mysticism in Religion*, p. 72.
9. Dickie, *God Is Light*, p. 47.
10. Hepburn, *Christianity and Paradox*, p. 17.
11. Baillie, *God Was in Christ*, p. 108.
12. *Ibid.*
13. *Ibid.*, p. 109.
14. *Ibid.*, pp. 109–110.
15. Farmer, *Revelation and Religion*, p. 169.
16. Watkin, "Consistent Empiricism," *The Hibbert Journal*, p. 33.
17. Campbell, *On Selfhood and Godhood*, p. 356.
18. *Ibid.*, p. 432.
19. Hume, *Dialogues Concerning Natural Religion*, p. 142.
20. Hepburn, *Christianity and Paradox*, p. 30.
21. *Ibid.*, p. 35.

Chapter 9. The "Improper" Functions of Theological Discourse

1. Hare, "Religion and Morals," *Faith and Logic, Oxford Essays in Philosophical Theology*, edited by Basil Mitchell (London: George Allen & Unwin Ltd., 1957), p. 179. This quotation and all others from the same book are used by special permission of the publisher.
2. Martin, "A Religious Way of Knowing," *New Essays in Philosophical Theology*, p. 78.
3. *Ibid.*, p. 80.
4. *Ibid.*, p. 82.
5. *Ibid.*, p. 85.
6. *Ibid.*
7. *Ibid.*, p. 86.
8. *Ibid.*, p. 87.
9. Glasgow, "Knowledge of God," *Philosophy*, p. 236.
10. Martin, "The Perfect Good," *New Essays in Philosophical Theology*, p. 219.
11. *Ibid.*, p. 215.
12. Ferré, *Christ and the Christian*; Baillie, *God Was in Christ*; DeWolf, *A Theology of the Living Church*; Aulén, *Christus Victor*; etc.
13. Flew, "Divine Omnipotence and Human Freedom," *New Essays in Philosophical Theology*, p. 149.
14. *Ibid.*
15. *Ibid.*, p. 150.
16. *Ibid.*
17. *Ibid.*
18. *Ibid.*, p. 152.
19. *Ibid.*, p. 153.

Chapter 10. The Familiar Functions of Theological Discourse

1. Coates, "God and the Positivists," *The Hibbert Journal*, p. 226.
2. *Ibid.*, p. 227.

3. MacKinnon, "Death," *New Essays in Philosophical Theology*, p. 262.
4. *Ibid.*, p. 263.
5. *Ibid.*
6. *Ibid.*, pp. 263–264.
7. Leon, "The Meaning of Religious Propositions," *The Hibbert Journal*, p. 151.
8. *Ibid.*
9. *Ibid.*, p. 153.
10. Allen, "The Arguments for God's Existence," *The Congregational Quarterly*, p. 348.
11. Braithwaite, *An Empiricist's View of the Nature of Religious Belief*, p. 11.
12. *Ibid.*
13. *Ibid.*
14. *Ibid.*, p. 15.
15. *Ibid.*, p. 19.
16. *Ibid.*, p. 34.
17. Mascall, *Words and Images*, p. 60.
18. *Ibid.*
19. Hepburn, *Christianity and Paradox*, p. 195.
20. *Ibid.*
21. *Ibid.*, p. 192.
22. Ewing, "Religious Assertions in the Light of Contemporary Philosophy," *Philosophy*, p. 207.
23. *Ibid.*, p. 211.
24. Whitely, "The Cognitive Factor in Religious Experience," p. 87.
25. Hare, *Faith and Logic*, p. 180.
26. *Ibid.*, pp. 180–181.
27. *Ibid.*, p. 189.
28. *Ibid.*, pp. 189–190.
29. *Ibid.*, p. 190.
30. *Ibid.*, p. 192.
31. Wisdom, "Gods," *Logic and Language*, First Series, p. 191.
32. *Ibid.*, p. 192.
33. *Ibid.*, p. 193.
34. *Ibid.*, p. 194.
35. *Ibid.*, p. 197.
36. *Ibid.*
37. *Ibid.*, p. 190.
38. *Ibid.*, p. 192.

Chapter 11. The Unique Functions of Theological Discourse

1. Allen, "The Great Argument," *The Expository Times*, pp. 116–118.
2. Smart, "The Existence of God," *New Essays in Philosophical Theology*, p. 40 (italics added).
3. *Ibid.*, p. 45.
4. Zuurdeeg, *An Analytical Philosophy of Religion*, p. 45.
5. *Ibid.*, p. 140.
6. *Ibid.*
7. *Ibid.*, p. 56.
8. *Ibid.*, p. 64.
9. Ramsey, *Religious Language*, p. 29.

10. *Ibid.*, p. 37.
11. *Ibid.*, pp. 27–28.
12. MacIntyre, "The Logical Status of Religious Belief," *Metaphysical Beliefs*, p. 185.
13. *Ibid.*, p. 193.
14. *Ibid.*, p. 199.
15. *Ibid.*, p. 202.
16. *Ibid.*
17. Crombie, "The Possibility of Theological Statements," *Faith and Logic*, p. 60.
18. *Ibid.*, pp. 70–71.
19. *Ibid.*, p. 81.
20. *Ibid.*

Chapter 12. The Manifold Logic of Theism

1. Strawson, *Introduction to Logical Theory*, p. 230.
2. Ryle, *Dilemmas*, p. 117.
3. See Gilkey, *Maker of Heaven and Earth*.
4. Ryle, *Dilemmas*, p. 126.
5. For a fuller treatment see my "Is Language about God Fraudulent?" pp. 351–360.
6. Hodges, *Languages, Standpoints and Attitudes*, p. 8.
7. *Ibid.*, p. 9.
8. Crombie, *Faith and Logic*, p. 31.
9. Ducasse, *A Philosophical Scrutiny of Religion*, pp. 131–132.
10. Compare Whitehead, *Process and Reality*, Chap. I.
11. Emmet, *The Nature of Metaphysical Thinking*, p. 4.
12. Williams, "Metaphysical Arguments," *The Nature of Metaphysics*, p. 60.

INDEX